the MEDITERRANEAN pantry

Aglaia Kremezi

Photographs by Martin Brigdale

the
MEDITERRANEAN
pantry

CREATING AND USING CONDIMENTS AND SEASONINGS

 ARTISAN *New York*

Editor: Ann ffolliott
Production Director: Hope Koturo

Published in 1994 by Artisan,
a division of Workman Publishing Company, Inc.
708 Broadway, New York, NY 10003

Library of Congress Cataloging-in-Publication Data
Kremezi, Aglaia.
The Mediterranean pantry: creating and using condi-
ments and seasonings / by Aglaia Kremezi: pho-
tographs by Martin Brigdale.
  Includes bibliographical references and index.
  ISBN 1-885183-02-X
    1. Condiments—Mediterranean Region.
2. Spices—Mediterranean Region. 3. Cookery,
Mediterranean. I. Title.
TX819.A1K74   1994
641.6 382 091822—dc20   94-11419

Printed in Japan
First Printing 1994
10 9 8 7 6 5 4 3 2 1

To Anna, Lenio, and Electra

Contents

Introduction

Even in this day of huge supermarkets and one-stop shopping, many people around the Mediterranean like to prepare their own fig jam and Morello cherry preserves, their own homemade tomato and hot chili pepper paste. They also prefer to cure their own olives and to dry their own grapes, figs, and tomatoes, to name but a few of the preparations that stock a typical Mediterranean pantry. I wrote this book because I wanted to share with you these delicious pantry items. Mediterranean cooks make the most of the best seasonal produce, often using simple local techniques that I hope will add a new zest to your everyday cooking.

You don't have to cook Tunisian to use harissa, the tastiest and most fragrant of hot pepper pastes, and you needn't necessarily cook Spanish to add Romesco Sauce, the versatile tomato sauce with a deep flavor, to any dish.

While compiling these recipes, I thought about modern, busy lives and cooks who crave tasty and healthy homemade food but cannot, on the average day, spend a lot of time in the kitchen. I collected recipes from all over the Mediterranean region—from old ladies in Astypalaia, a remote Greek island, to bakers in isolated mountainous villages in Crete, and from Berbers who live in houses dug into stone hills on the edge of the Sahara, to sophisticated chefs from Barcelona, and from ancient Greek and Roman papyruses to old Ottoman cooking manuscripts. I have chosen recipes for foods that can be prepared weeks or months in advance and can be served either by themselves or as flavorful additions to salads, steamed vegetables, pastas, risottos, and hot and cold fish, poultry, and meat dishes.

I hope that these recipes will help you serve such interesting snacks or appetizers as Grilled Vegetables in Olive Oil (page 102), Fried Artichokes with Garlic in Olive Oil (page 97), Yogurt Cheese in Olive Oil with Chili Pepper and Herbs (page 98), and Eggplant, Pepper, and Walnut Spread (page 77) at a moment's notice. You can now have on hand the main ingredients for such interesting main dishes as Pasta with Grilled Peppers (page 100), Pasta with Olive Oil, Anchovies, and Fennel (page 23), and Artichoke and Leek Risotto (page 71).

Because most modern kitchens are not very large and cooking as well as storage spaces are usually limited, I have chosen to keep the recipe yields in this book relatively small. However, if you want to double or triple a recipe, go right ahead. Pantry items also make excellent gifts for friends and relatives. Instead of buying a bottle of wine or liqueur to bring at a dinner party, you can offer your flavorful homemade ratafia (pages 32 and 33) or thyme liqueur (page 36). You can also make a nice gift box filled with paximadia, the crunchy savory biscuits (pages 58, 62, and 63) or with sweet biscotti (pages 47, 55, and 56), to name but a few of the prepared foods and drinks that will make your friends particularly happy. Search out particularly pretty jars for your gifts (see Mail-Order Sources, page 134).

PRESERVED FOOD IN HISTORY

It is amazing how little the basic methods for preserving food have changed through the ages. Ancient Greeks and Romans used salt, vinegar, olive oil, honey, all kinds of spices, wood smoke, and the powerful heat of the blazing Mediterranean sun to prevent foods from spoiling and to keep them for the next season. They didn't have refrigeration, and they surely didn't have the luxury of being able to throw away food that had gone bad. Food was expensive and scarce so they had to come up with effective ways to use every bit of the edibles they bought or cultivated.

Furthermore, until the beginning of this century, few prepared foods were available in stores. Sauces, condiments, jams, marmalades, and pickles—used to complement and enrich the everyday table—had to be made at home by each family. In most rural areas housewives were also obliged to bake the family's breads.

In his book *On Agriculture,* the Roman statesman Cato (3rd century B.C.) advises on how to cure olives: ". . .crush them and place them in vinegar, olive oil, and salt and add fennel and lentiscus. . ." In Greece and many other Mediterranean countries, green olives are still prepared in exactly the same way, although lentiscus, a fragrant shrub of the wild pistachio family (the same family of plants that gives us its dried saps as mastic and its crushed berries as sumac) is not used anymore.

In Apicius's *De Re Coquinaria (On Cooking)*, a compilation of classical Greek and Roman recipes written during the last years B.C. or first A.D., there is a recipe for preserving turnips that reads: "Mix mustard seeds with honey, vinegar, and salt and pour over turnip. . ." While the honey has been replaced by sugar in modern times, little else about the ingredients or method differs.

In Tunisia today, a primeval gruel, made from roasted and then ground sorghum seasoned with dried fruit, honey, salt, and coriander, is served for breakfast. It must not be very different than the barley gruel (prepared in exactly the same way) that was the staple food of ancient Greeks and Romans. Also still alive in the cuisines of the Middle East and North Africa are the marvelous ancient spice mixtures, such as Zaatar (page 42) and Bharat (page 44), as well as the combination of sweet and savory flavors, which probably aren't very different from the foods our ancestors savored in antiquity.

THE PANTRY TODAY

In the latter half of the twentieth century the pantry has, for the most part, come to mean the refrigerator, where cold temperatures help us to keep foods for long periods of time. Although now a tremendous variety of commercially prepared foods line our supermarket shelves, few are equal in quality to the homemade ones. Fortunately, however, today farmers' markets are full of delicious supplies of organically grown vegetables, fruits, and herbs, and even local cheeses and using these high-quality seasonal produce, you can prepare the best homemade preserves.

Although salted sardines and other local dried or smoked fish form a major part of most Mediterranean pantries, recipes for them are not included in this book because neither the fish used in the Mediterranean nor any close equivalents are readily available outside of that region.

FRUITS, VEGETABLES, AND HERBS

All kinds of seasonal vegetables, often grown in the garden, play a crucial role in Mediterranean cooking. Those vegetables are cooked by themselves or complimented with foods made from grains—such as pasta, couscous, rice or simply bread—and small amounts of meat, make the traditional dishes of the region.

In poor villages in Asia Minor, or in the Greek islands, you will find long eggplants, okra, and string beans, passed through a piece of string and hanged to dry so they can be used in the winter. In the mountainous villages of Epirus, in northwestern Greece, even the different varieties of wild greens that people gather from the hills are dried in bunches, so they can be available in the snowy winter months for the preparation of the local wild greens pies.

Tomatoes and peppers came to Europe from the New World and have played an indispensable role in the Mediterranean diet since approximately the end of the seventeenth century. Today, rather than drying tomatoes in the sun, I suggest drying them (and other vegetables) in a low oven (see page 70). Use only fresh, fleshy vine-ripened plum tomatoes; if perfect tomatoes are not available, opt for the packaged Italian sun-dried tomatoes sold in specialty stores and some supermarkets.

Hot chili peppers, very easily cultivated in the Mediterranean, are the primary ingredient in both Harissa (page 83) and Hrous (page 86), two fiery pastes from the Magreb (Arab North Africa). Don't limit use of them to Tunisian and Moroccan dishes; use them to add zest and extra dimension to soups and stews, marinades and rubs for meat and poultry, and raw and cooked sauces.

Mediterranean pickles are strongly flavored, with a vivid vinegar taste. They are often served as appetizers, accompanied by strong, sweet drinks, such as pastis, ouzo, or raki. They are not served with wine because their strong acidic flavor would kill even the strongest wine. If you prefer sweeter pickles, you can increase the amount of sugar or honey, but the balance should always be toward the acidic.

The most popular Mediterranean herbs—oregano, savory, thyme, and rosemary—are almost exclusively used in their sun-dried form. Herbs are also burned to fill rooms with their aroma and create the right mood (see page 73). Because these herbs do not have the same flavor when cultivated in other parts of the world, it is worth finding a source for the Mediterranean variety (see Mail-Order Sources, page 134).

On rooftops of Sicilian, Greek, Spanish, Middle Eastern, and North African houses you are still likely to find grapes, figs, apricots, dates, and plums drying in the sun with the tomatoes, peppers, and homemade liqueurs and sauces that are left there to macerate.

Fruits are very important and are always present on a Mediterranean table, either fresh or dried. Figs, grapes, and dates were extremely important for the inhabitants of the region from the dawn of civilization, as we learn from ancient texts and the Bible. With those dried fruits and nuts, traditional sweets such as the delicious Dried Fig and Apricot Balls (page 69) or sweet and sour preserves such as Sweet and Sour Dried Figs (page 81) are made. But dried fruits are also used in savory dishes, especially in the delicious North African couscous and tajines.

FLAVORED OILS AND HOMEMADE DRINKS

Olive oil was and still is the basic fat used in most Mediterranean countries. Vegetables, fish, and meat are cooked with it, while in many parts of Greece olive oil is even used in baking. But from ancient times olive oil has also helped people preserve foods, as it forms an air-tight seal above other liquids, such as vinegar and salt brines, preventing the growth of molds.

Olive trees are ubiquitous to the region, and they give their silvery green color to the soft hills and the small plains of Greece, Southern Italy, Sicily, Spain, and the south of France. They have even adapted themselves to such harsh conditions as the semi-desert environment of north Africa.

In every region people have their own particular preferences for the fruits of this ancient tree: Some choose green rather than black olives, and cure and dress them with such diverse condiments as orange juice and zest and harissa sauce (page 91).

Flavored, fragrant oils were another ancient condiment, dating at least from the thirteenth century B.C. Oils scented with herbs and flowers, stored in special small clay jars, were essential accessories for ancient athletes, because olive oil was used as a cosmetic then. It is difficult for us today to distinguish which flavored oils were used for food and which for cosmetic purposes from the ancient lists found in the palaces of Knossos, in Crete.

From these Minoan lists comes my Olive Oil with Capers, to which I added Chili Peppers (page 20), while *liquamen* or *garum,* the ancient fermented fish sauce, has inspired the anchovy flavored olive oil (page 22) as well as the traditional Sicilian Pasta with Olive Oil, Anchovies, and Fennel (page 23) that can be made with it.

In France, Italy, Spain, and Greece, many families make their own wine in barrels in shady backyards and basements and even in garages and on balconies. Grape must (freshly pressed grape juice) can be purchased in late summer and early fall from nearby vineyards and from then on people usually let nature take its course. Homemade wine, the people who produce it will tell you, is light and pure and will never give you a hangover because no chemical additives are used.

Not everyone in the world can produce his or her own wine, of course, but a very easy beverage that everyone can create at home is the strong but fruity Ratafia (pages 32 and 33). This dessert drink is a favorite among wine producers, who make it with their most fragrant grape must, usually for consumption at home with family and friends. The principle is quite simple: Alcohol in the form of brandy, eau-de-vie, or vodka is added to fresh grape juice (stopping the fermentation process), sugar is added if the fruit is not sweet enough, and the mixture is left to macerate for 4 weeks. Ratafia de Champagne, produced in the Champagne region of France from the same grapes that are used to make the most precious of all wines, is one excellent example. Another is the famous Vin de Liqueur from the Greek island of Samos, produced from the very sweet and fragrant variety of grapes that grow there.

Ratafia can be made with all kinds of fruits or even different fruit combinations. My favorite is Quince Ratafia (page 32), but I also love Grape and Apricot Ratafia (page 33), which can be made with any kind of grapes, even the ones found in your local supermarket.

Not all of the people who inhabit the countries around the Mediterranean drink alcoholic beverages, which are forbidden under the religious laws of Islam. For that reason another kind of drink, made from sweet concentrated fruit and herb syrups, is popular in Turkey, the Middle East, and North Africa. One of the most interesting combinations is the ancient *oxymel* (page 39), once made with vinegar and honey, today made with vinegar and sugar.

Almonds, a very much appreciated product of the region, are also used to make drinks, both alcoholic and non-alcoholic. Almond milk and a magnificent almond liqueur called Crema di Mandorla are favorite Sicilian Drinks. In Greece and the Middle East, almond syrup (page 30) is diluted with ice cold water and offered at very special occasions, including engagements and weddings.

BISCOTTI AND PAXIMADIA

Bread is still the staple food around the Mediterranean. Because fresh bread can't be made quickly, people like to have tins of tasty, home-baked savory biscuits around the house to dip in milk or coffee for breakfast, nibble as a snack, or eat at lunch or dinner with cheese, salads, soups, and stews. Italians call these biscuits *pane biscottato* (twice-baked bread) and Greeks call them *paximadia*. The principle is the same: Bread is sliced while fresh, then baked again in a very low oven until completely dry.

These dried breads were for centuries the staple food of the Mediterranean people. In places where wood for burning in the oven was scarce, dried breads were the ideal solution because they were baked in bulk every two or three months. For the same reason, sailors continue to this day to take them on their long voyages. Also, as an anthropologist friend pointed out to me, *paximadia* were an economical solution for people who had limited amounts of food. Unlike fresh bread, which was gobbled up quickly, these dried biscuits lasted for a long time.

In ancient times *paximadia* were most commonly made from barley flour and left to dry in the sun; when ready to eat they were dipped in water, drizzled with olive oil, and combined with olives, salted and dried fish, cheese, or simply onions and garlic. Nearly the same barley biscuits (page 58) continued be the basic food of the Greeks who lived in Crete and the other islands of the Aegean Sea until the early 1960s.

Greek women have developed several techniques to make these biscuits crunchy and light. Starting with their basic bread recipe, they increase the amount of leavening (almost always sourdough in rural Greece) and of sugar or honey and olive oil, making a softer dough, and they knead it longer. I have often heard village women say that, unlike dough for bread, the one for *paximadia* needs to be very well calculated in advance because if you add flour or water while you knead, the biscuits will be hard, but I have found this to be completely unfounded.

Some old recipes for *paximadia* call for several rising times, sometimes over the course of three days. Flour is gradually added to the sourdough, which is then left to rest overnight. The next day more flour is kneaded in and left for three to four hours. This process is repeated numerous times. This is a clever technique, especially because in the old days when women used ten to twenty pounds of flour each time they baked these biscuits, the large quantities made the dough very hard to knead properly.

Biscotti, a close relation to *paximadia*, are sweet, much richer varieties of dried bread. Americans have learned to love them from the Italians. In Greece, *biskotakia* or *koulourakia,* as we call them, are often shaped into tiny crowns instead of being baked in a loaf and then cut diagonally. In this book I have included three recipes for *biscotti:* the first is a very old Cretan one that contains wine, orange juice and zest, and spices (page 47), the second uses yogurt and whole pistachios (page 55), and the third is made by baking slices of the traditional Greek Easter bread, very similar to the Italian Easter Panetone (page 56).

BASIC PRESERVING PRINCIPLES

⚘ Food spoils because it is attacked by microorganisms. Most microorganisms need air to survive so by preventing food from coming into contact with air, we keep it from spoiling. Olive oil on top of a paste, spread, or sauce also prevents food from coming into contact with air.

⚘ Vinegar, large amounts of salt, sugar, and alcohol (over 18 percent) discourage the development of most microorganisms so we can preserve vegetables and fruits in vinegar, salted brine, syrup, or strong dessert wines.

⚘ No microorganism can live without water. That is why we dry vegetables, fruits, bread, and meat that we want to preserve.

⚘ Microorganisms can also be killed by heat. By boiling filled and sealed jars and bottles in a canning kettle for about 10 minutes, using a method called a hot-water bath, we can keep conserved foods at room temperature for months.

⚘ Microorganisms take longer to develop in the cool atmosphere of the refrigerator, which means that such foods as sauces, vegetables in olive oil, and spreads can be kept in the refrigerator for extended but not unlimited periods of time.

EQUIPMENT

Following is a list of cooking equipment that will help you achieve success with the recipes in this book.

⚘ NONREACTIVE PANS to cook preserves and also to make vinegar brines.

⚘ SEVERAL WOODEN SPOONS to stir the food while it is cooking. Because wooden spoons have the tendency to absorb flavors and smells, it is a good idea to separate the ones you use for sweets from the ones you use for strongly flavored pickles and sauces.

§ THE SPECIALLY DESIGNED CLAMPED ALL-GLASS JARS AND BOTTLES WITH A RUBBER RING AND THE CLASSIC MASON JARS (not old mustard or mayonnaise jars because their lids corrode easily, especially when they come in contact with vinegar). Jars and bottles should be washed thoroughly with soap, rinsed with almost boiling water, then left to dry and sterilize in a 200–225°F oven for about 20 minutes. Warm food can be added to the jars immediately after taking the jars out of the oven, but cold foods should only be added after the jars have cooled because the sudden change in temperature could cause the warm jars to break. Leave about ½ inch of space at the top of filled preserving jars and bottles, especially if you plan to process them in a hot water bath. Wipe the top of the jars with a clean cloth dampened in very warm water.

§ A JAR FUNNEL to fill jars without making a mess.

§ A CANDY THERMOMETER if you plan to make jams and fruit preserves. Choose a high-quality one; it can also be used to measure the temperature of oil when deep-frying.

§ GOOD KNIVES for slicing and peeling various vegetables and fruit and a good bread knife to slice breads and cake for *paximadia* and *biscotti*.

§ A ZESTER to be used with oranges and lemons.

§ HIGH-QUALITY, PREFERABLY ELECTRONIC, KITCHEN SCALES, especially if you plan to make fresh herbs preserved in salt (pages 94 and 95).

§ LABELS AND WATERPROOF MARKING PENS. Always write the contents and date of preparation on all jars and bottles. Check the recipe to find out its maximum storage time and add an expiration date to the label.

WARNING SIGNS

§ Some foods that are kept in the refrigerator will solidify, especially if they contain lots of olive oil. This is completely natural. Remove the portion of food desired one hour before serving and let it sit at room temperature.

§ Sauces containing vinegar or lemon and olive oil will separate. Always shake well before using.

❧ Although maximum storage times for the recipes in this book take into account the worst case scenarios, accidents may occur. Smell all foods before serving. If the smell is bad, discard the food. Also look carefully at the food before serving. Foam or bubbles tell you that the food has spoiled. Discard it immediately. Molds that develop on the surface of some preserved foods are rarely dangerous. Often you need only remove the layer of mold before safely consuming the food that lies underneath.

IN BOTTLES

Olive Oil with Capers and Chili Peppers

THE SECRET OF making an excellent flavored olive oil is starting with the best and freshest aromatic herbs and good-quality extra-virgin olive oil.

Use Olive Oil with Capers and Chili Pepper to flavor salads and steamed or grilled vegetables. Mayonnaise made with this oil has an exquisite taste.

1 jar best-quality large capers in salt, not in vinegar (See Mail-Order Sources, page 134)
2–3 fresh hot chili peppers
2 cups fruity extra-virgin olive oil

Rinse the capers in running water and drain well on paper towels. Chop 2 tablespoons of the capers and place them in a clean and absolutely dry 2-cup bottle. Add the remaining capers and the chili peppers and fill the bottle with olive oil. Cover and keep in a cool, dark place for a week, shaking from time to time, before using.

Olive Oil with Capers and Chili Pepper will keep for 3 to 6 months in a cool, dark place. Makes 2 cups.

OPPOSITE
Olive Oil with Rosemary and Pink Peppercorns, Olive Oil with Capers and Chili Peppers, and Olive Oil with Anchovies and Chili Peppers

Olive Oil with Anchovies and Chili Peppers

Garum, also called *liquamen,* was the favorite sauce of both the ancient Greeks and Romans—as ubiquitous in those days as ketchup is today. It was made from small fish and fish guts that were left to macerate in the sun with salt, vinegar, and spices. This strong sauce was used to flavor all kinds of foods, including vegetables, dried beans, meat, and fish.

It is believed that the anchovy sauces we encounter today in the south of Italy, and especially in Sicily, have their roots in this ancient sauce, as does the old English standby, Worcestershire.

Use Olive Oil with Anchovies and Chili Peppers to dress tomato salads and steamed or grilled vegetables. It is particularly good with steamed cauliflower and broccoli.

4 anchovy fillets in olive oil
1 fresh chili pepper, bruised
2 cups extra-virgin olive oil

Drain the anchovies and pat dry with paper towels.

Chop 1 of the anchovies and place it in a clean and absolutely dry 2-cup bottle. Add the whole anchovies and the bruised chili pepper. Fill the bottle with the olive oil, cover, and let stand in a dark place for a week, shaking from time to time, before using.

Olive Oil with Anchovies and Chili Peppers will keep for 3 to 6 months stored in a cool, dark place.

Makes 2 cups.

Pasta with Olive Oil, Anchovies, and Fennel

THIS SAUCE IS BEST on *bucatini* (or *perciatelli*), a factory-made pasta that looks like thick spaghetti but has a hollow core.

2 fennel bulbs, 1 sliced and 1 chopped

1 pound bucatini, perciatelli, or spaghetti

2 tablespoons olive oil

3–4 garlic cloves, chopped

⅔ cup chopped fresh wild fennel or fennel tops

2 anchovy fillets, chopped

⅓–½ teaspoon red pepper flakes

⅓ cup Olive Oil with Anchovies and Chili Peppers (previous page)

Freshly ground black pepper and sea salt

Fill a large pot with water and bring to a boil. Add the sliced fennel bulb and the *bucatini* and cook until the pasta is al dente, approximately 10 minutes. Meanwhile, place the 2 tablespoons olive oil in a large, nonreactive, heavy skillet. Add the chopped fennel bulb and sauté over medium heat for about 3 minutes. Add the garlic, half of the wild fennel, the chopped anchovies, and the red pepper flakes. Cook, stirring, for 6 to 8 minutes, or until the greens are tender.

Drain the pasta, reserving a little of the cooking liquid. Chop the boiled fennel and add it to the sauce along with ¼ cup of the cooking liquid and the drained pasta. Drizzle with the Olive Oil with Anchovies and Chili Peppers. Add the remaining chopped fennel and toss well. Taste, adjust the seasonings, and serve at once.

Serves 4 to 6.

Olive Oil with Rosemary and Pink Peppercorns

Use this oil to season steamed potatoes and grilled meat, poultry, or fish.

3–4 branches fresh rosemary
2 tablespoons pink peppercorns
2 cups fruity extra-virgin olive oil

Rinse and dry the rosemary branches. Place them in a clean and absolutely dry 2-cup bottle with the peppercorns. Fill with the olive oil. Cover and keep in a cool, dark place for a week, shaking from time to time (see Note), before using.

Olive Oil with Rosemary and Red Peppercorns will keep for 3 to 6 months stored in a cool, dark place.

Makes 2 cups.

NOTE: Taste the oil at the end of the week; if you want a stronger flavor, pass the oil through a sieve, discard the used rosemary and peppercorns, and repeat the procedure using fresh rosemary and peppercorns. Leave the herbs and spices in the bottle as you use the oil.

THIS LUXURIOUS OIL will taste best if you make it with fresh truffles, but it can also be made with good-quality whole truffles preserved in brine.

To make truffle-flavored *bruschetta,* toast slices of country bread, then, while they are still warm, rub a halved garlic clove over them and drizzle with Olive Oil with Truffles. Serve as an appetizer.

For a real treat, mix a few tablespoons of the oil with butter when making scrambled eggs.

1 small jar (about 2–3) truffles

1 cup fruity extra-virgin olive oil

½ teaspoon fresh, coarsely ground black pepper, or to taste

Thinly slice the truffles. In a small frying pan, warm 4 tablespoons of the olive oil over low heat, then add the sliced truffles and the pepper. Cook gently for a few minutes, watching carefully so that the truffles don't brown. Don't let the mixture get too hot. Remove from the heat, let cool a little, and mix with the remaining olive oil. Pour into a clean and dry 1-cup bottle and let stand for 3 to 5 days, shaking from time to time. Store in a cool, dark place.

Olive Oil with Truffles will keep for 6 months to a year.

Makes 1 cup.

Sicilian Garlic and Mint Sauce

I TASTED this simple and delicious sauce on grilled fish in a famous restaurant called Jonico in Syracuse. The owner, Pascualino Juidice, told me that it is also served with oven-roasted rabbit. I have found that it tastes better if made in advance so the garlic and mint have time to macerate.

Serve Sicilian Garlic and Mint Sauce with grilled or fried fish and with grilled rabbit or chicken.

3 large garlic cloves, quartered

1 small dried chili pepper, cut in half lengthwise

⅔ cup good-quality red wine vinegar

3 teaspoons crumbled dried mint leaves

1⅓ cups fruity extra-virgin olive oil

Drop the garlic into a clean 2-cup bottle. Add the chili pepper and pour in the vinegar. Add half the mint, cover the bottle, shake well, and leave for about 24 hours. In the beginning the flavorings will float on the surface of the vinegar, but after a day they will sink to the bottom of the bottle. After the flavorings have sunk to the bottom, add the olive oil and the remaining mint. Shake well and let stand for about 3 to 4 days, shaking once or twice a day, before using.

Sicilian Garlic and Mint Sauce will keep for 2 to 3 months in a cool, dark place. Shake well just before using.

Makes 2 cups.

THIS IS MY ATTEMPT to create an interesting vinegar that resembles balsamic vinegar. It has a deep flavor and a woody aroma, and makes an excellent addition to any salad of raw or cooked vegetables.

3 tablespoons thyme-flavored honey

1½ cups raisins

5 dried figs, chopped

2 cups sweet red wine, such as Greek
　　Mavrodaphne

2 cups good-quality red wine vinegar

1 cup good-quality white wine vinegar

About 1 cup total of different kinds of fresh
　　wood chips, such as pine, oak, maple, apple
　　wood, and walnut (tied in a double layer of
　　cheesecloth)

In a nonreactive saucepan, combine the honey, 1 cup of the raisins, half of the chopped figs, and the sweet wine. Bring to a boil, lower the heat, and simmer, stirring from time to time, until reduced to about 1 cup. Pass the mixture through a fine sieve into a bowl and discard the figs and raisins.

Tie the remaining raisins and figs in a piece of cheesecloth. Combine the flavored wine with the red and white wine vinegars in a clean 1½-quart jar. Add both cheesecloth packages (the dried fruit in one and the wood chips in the other). Cover and let stand for 3 to 4 weeks, shaking from time to time.

Discard both cheesecloth packages, pass the vinegar through a fine sieve into a bowl, then transfer to a 1-quart bottle and cover tightly.

Honeyed Wine Vinegar will keep for 1 year stored in a cool, dark place.

Makes 1 quart.

Of THE INFINITE VARIETIES of easy-to-make flavored vinegars, this is one of my favorites. If a fragrant peach is not available, dried apricots or other fresh fruits such as pears, strawberries, or raspberries can be substituted. Also, instead of fresh rosemary, try dried Mediterranean oregano, thyme, or savory—herbs that I have found to be most robust in their dried form, as opposed to fresh.

Use this vinegar to dress salads, especially delicate ones that include fruit.

OPPOSITE
Peach and Rosemary Vinegar and Honeyed Wine Vinegar

1 fresh peach or 4 dried apricots, coarsely chopped

2 sprigs fresh rosemary

2 cups good-quality cider vinegar

Place the chopped peach or dried apricots in a 3-cup bottle with a large opening. Add the rosemary and pour in the vinegar. Cover, shake well, and set aside for about 3 to 4 weeks, shaking at least once every day.

If you have used fresh fruit, pass the vinegar through a fine-meshed sieve lined with cheesecloth. If you want to intensify the rosemary flavor, replace the rosemary sprigs with fresh ones.

Peach and Rosemary Vinegar will keep for more than a year in a cool, dark place.

Makes 2 cups.

Almond Syrup

OPPOSITE
*Almond Syrup and
Mint Oxymel Syrup*

Aｌｍｏｎｄ ｍｉｌｋ and a magnificent almond liqueur, called Crema di Mandorla, are favorite Sicilian drinks. In Greece and the Middle East, we dilute our precious almond syrup (called *soumada* in Greek) with ice-cold water and offer it at weddings, engagements, and other special occasions. At one time this expensive delicacy was given to nursing women as it was believed to help them produce more milk.

To serve, stir 2 to 3 tablespoons of the syrup into a large glass filled with ½ to ⅔ cup water and some ice cubes. If you like, add a little Crema di Mandorla.

You can also use this almond syrup as a sauce for chocolate ice cream or as a flavoring when making almond ice cream.

1½ cups blanched and skinned almonds (about 8½ ounces)	4 cups warm water
½ teaspoon almond extract	3 cups sugar

Soak the almonds in 2 cups warm water for 4 hours or overnight. Place the soaked almonds with their liquid in the bowl of a food processor and process at high speed until you obtain a fine, milky meal.

Line a fine-meshed sieve with a piece of wet cheesecloth and strain the milky almond meal through it and into a bowl. Gather the corners of the cheesecloth and press hard to extract all of the liquid. Place the solids in a separate bowl and pour 1 cup warm water over them. Stir with a fork, then strain again through the cheesecloth-lined sieve into the bowl of almond milk. Press hard to extract as much almond milk as possible. Repeat once more, soaking the remaining solids in the last cup of warm water, then straining and pressing the solids in the cheesecloth.

You should now have 4 cups almond milk and some wet chopped almond meal (see Note). Place the almond milk and sugar in a nonreactive saucepan and simmer for 45 minutes to 1 hour, until the syrup thickens, reaching 220–230 °F. on a candy thermometer.

Pass the syrup through a fine sieve into a clean and absolutely dry 3-cup bottle. Seal, let cool, and keep at room temperature.

Almond Syrup will keep for up to a year.

Makes about 3 cups.

ｎｏｔｅ: Spread the chopped almond meal on a baking sheet and place in a warm oven (175 °F.) until completely dry. Keep in a bag or glass jar to use in sweets, cookies, or sauces.

Quince Ratafia

QUINCES ARE MY FAVORITE autumn fruits—so fragrant and versatile for everybody who is willing to invest a little effort to bring out their best qualities.

Ancient Greeks used them to make perfumes, and today people of the Mediterranean love them baked, made into sweet preserves, or cooked with meat and poultry. Choose the most fragrant fruits, even if they are green, handling them carefully because they bruise easily; store them in a basket in a cool place until they turn yellow.

Serve Quince Ratafia as a dessert drink, neat in small liqueur glasses or with crushed ice in wine glasses or champagne flutes.

2–3 quinces (1½ pounds)	2 cinnamon sticks, each 1 inch long
1–1⅓ cups sugar	4–5 cups vodka or eau-de-vie

Wash and dry the quinces, rubbing them with a soft kitchen towel to get rid of their fuzz. Using a large chef's knife, quarter the quinces and drop the pieces into the bowl of a food processor, seeds and skins included. Process, pulsing the machine on and off, until you obtain coarsely chopped fruit. You should have about 4 cups.

Divide the chopped quinces between two 1-quart jars or bottles with large openings. Add ½ to ⅔ cup sugar to each bottle, according to how sweet you like your drinks. Add 1 cinnamon stick followed by 2 to 2½ cups vodka or eau-de-vie to each bottle. Cover and shake well.

Leave in a cool, dark place for 2 to 4 weeks, shaking once a day for the first week so that the sugar dissolves completely. The longer you leave the *ratafia,* the mellower it will become.

Discard the cinnamon sticks and strain the *ratafia* through a fine-meshed sieve lined with a double layer of cheesecloth into a bowl. Gather the ends of the cloth and press well to extract all the liquid. Pour the *ratafia* into a 3-cup bottle, seal, and keep in a dark, cool place or in the refrigerator.

Quince Ratafia keeps for years.

Makes 4 to 5 cups.

CHOOSE THE FRESHEST and most fragrant grapes you can find to produce the best *ratafia*. This recipe requires less sugar than the quince recipe because grapes and apricots are naturally much sweeter than quinces.

Serve Grape and Apricot Ratafia as a dessert drink, neat in a small liqueur glass or with crushed ice in a wine glass or champagne flute.

OVERLEAF
*Dried Apricots
in Samos Vin
de Liqueur,
Grape and Apricot
Ratafia, Thyme
Liqueur, and
Quince Ratafia*

2 pounds grapes, preferably fragrant (any kind will do)
1 cup good-quality, organic dried apricots
  (see recipe introduction on page 115)

2 tablespoons–⅓ cup sugar
3–4 cups vodka or eau-de-vie

Wash and dry the grapes. Discard the stems and place the grapes in a food processor. Process, pulsing the machine on and off, until you obtain a juicy pulp. With a pair of kitchen scissors, cut the dried apricots into small pieces.

Place the grape pulp and apricots in a 6-cup jar or bottle, add 2 tablespoons to ⅓ cup sugar (depending on how sweet you like your drinks), and top with the vodka or eau-de-vie to fill the jar. Shake well and leave in a cool, dark place for 2 to 4 weeks, shaking once a day for the first week so that the sugar will dissolve completely. The longer you leave it, the mellower it will become.

Strain the *ratafia* through a fine-meshed sieve lined with a double layer of cheesecloth into a bowl. Gather the ends of the cloth and press well to extract all juices. Pour the *ratafia* into a bottle, seal, and keep in a cool, dark place or in the refrigerator.

Grape and Apricot Ratafia will keep for years.

Makes about 6 cups.

Morello Cherry Liqueur

Wᴴᴱɴ ɪ ᴡᴀꜱ ᴀ ᴄʜɪʟᴅ, every Greek family made its own special cherry liqueur, which was served to guests who dropped in for a visit.

Homemade liqueurs taste so much fresher than commercial ones that it is worth the small effort needed to make them. The best is undeniably cherry liqueur, produced in late June or early July when Morello cherries—a variety of sour cherries that is very popular in Europe—are at their peak. If Morello cherries are not available, you can make the liqueur with any kind of sour or sweet cherries. Good-quality dried cherries are also suitable.

2 pounds fresh Morello (or other variety)
   fresh cherries or 1 pound dried cherries
Approximately 1½ pounds sugar
1 pint pure-grain alcohol

1 pint good-quality brandy
1 cinnamon stick, 2 inches long
3–5 whole cloves

Wash and remove the stems from the cherries. Place a layer of cherries in a 2-quart jar and cover with a ½-inch layer of sugar. Repeat until all of the cherries and sugar have been used. Fill the jar with the pure-grain alcohol and close tightly. Place in a sunny spot and leave to macerate for about 4 weeks.

Add the brandy, cinnamon, and cloves to the jar. Close tightly and let stand another 2 weeks, shaking every so often.

Strain and serve, adding 1 or 2 cherries to each glass of liqueur, or store in a cool, dark place.

Morello Cherry Liqueur will keep for about a year.

Makes about 3 cups.

Thyme Liqueur

Aᴄᴄᴏʀᴅɪɴɢ ᴛᴏ ᴛʜᴇ ꜰʀᴇɴᴄʜ, thyme tisane is an excellent treatment for a hangover. Thyme is also thought to be an excellent digestive, which makes this fragrant thyme liqueur from the South of France the perfect conclusion to a Mediterranean dinner. Always make this recipe with thyme of excellent quality—either wild thyme or dried Mediterranean thyme.

⅔ cup flowered wild thyme branches or dried
   Mediterranean thyme
1 quart flavorless vodka or eau-de-vie

¾ cup sugar
1 branch fresh thyme

Place the thyme in a bottle that holds more than 1 quart. Add the vodka or eau-de-vie and let it stand for 5 weeks, shaking every 2 or 3 days. Add the sugar and shake well. Let stand for another week, shaking at least once every day. The sugar should dissolve by the end of the week.

Pass the liqueur through a double layer of moistened cheesecloth and transfer to a 1-quart bottle. Add the branch of fresh thyme and seal. Store in a dark, cool place.

Thyme Liqueur will keep for more than 1 year.

Makes 1 quart.

ᴠᴀʀɪᴀᴛɪᴏɴ: To make Sage or Fennel Liqueur, substitute sage or wild fennel for the thyme. Both are delicious.

Mint Oxymel Syrup

Ancient greeks called this *oxymeli* (vinegar-honey), and this sweet and tangy drink was thought to be very refreshing. Although sugar has replaced honey, people continue to enjoy similar drinks today, especially in Muslim countries where alcoholic beverages are prohibited.

In a Turkish cookbook compiled by Turabi Efendi in 1862, I found a vinegar-sugar syrup called *oxymel* that was scented with sweet marjoram. Starting from that basic recipe I experimented with different quantities of sugar and vinegar, using marjoram, mint, and rose geranium as flavorings. My favorite was mint-flavored *oxymel,* but you can try the other herbs as well.

To serve, place 2 to 3 tablespoons in a glass, pour in very cold water and ice cubes, and decorate with a sprig of fresh mint.

4 cups water	1 cup distilled white vinegar
1 cup sugar	15–20 sprigs fresh mint

Bring the water and sugar to a boil in a nonreactive pan. Simmer for about 10 minutes, then add the vinegar. Continue simmering for another 15 minutes. Add the mint to the pan, and when the liquid starts to boil again, remove it from the heat and let cool. Remove and discard the sprigs of mint, pass the syrup through a fine sieve, and store in a bottle in the refrigerator.

Mint Oxymel Syrup will keep for 6 months in the refrigerator.

Makes 1 cup.

IN BOXES

Zaatar

THE LEBANESE believe that *zaatar,* a mixture of thyme, sumac, and sesame seeds, gives strength and clears the mind. For this reason, before leaving home on exam days all school-children eat a slice of bread spread with a mixture of *zaatar* and olive oil.

The red sour-tart little fruits of sumac (*Rhus corioria*) are a favorite Middle Eastern spice, especially in Lebanon. Sumac is part of the large wild pistachio family, which includes shrubs with small, hard, and very fragrant leaves that grow on the most dry and rocky Mediterranean shores. One very close relation to sumac is called *skinos* and is particularly common in Greece. Ancient Greeks used to flavor olive oil with branches of *skinos*. Mastic, the beloved Greek and Middle Eastern flavoring for breads and sweets, is the resin of another plant (*Pistacia lentiscus*) belonging to this family.

The traditional recipe for *zaatar* calls for thyme, but I have found that savory—which has an aroma similar to a combination of oregano and thyme—works much better.

To use, mix 1 to 2 tablespoons of *zaatar* with 1 to 2 tablespoons virgin olive oil and spread on warm toasted bread. Top with freshly ground black pepper and serve.

You can also top frozen or homemade pita breads with the *zaatar* and olive oil mixture before baking them in the oven.

½ cup excellent-quality Mediterranean savory
  (see Mail-Order Sources, page 134)
¼ cup sumac (see Mail-Order Sources, page 134)

½ teaspoon coarse sea salt
2 tablespoons sesame seed

Grind the savory, sumac, salt, and sesame seed in a spice grinder or clean coffee grinder until you obtain a fine powder. Keep in a sealed jar in a cool, dark, and dry place. *Zaatar* will begin to lose its flavor after 2 months.

Makes about ¾ cup.

I CALL THIS SPICY RUB North African because it contains such Tunisian and Moroccan spices as caraway, cumin, and turmeric in addition to *harissa,* the ubiquitous hot pepper paste that is found in all of the countries of the Magreb (Arab North Africa).

Rub poultry, lamb, beef, or pork two to three hours before grilling and leave at room temperature. Or mix 3 tablespoons of this rub with 3 tablespoons thick yogurt, baste the meat with the mixture, then cover and leave to marinate overnight in the refrigerator.

3 tablespoons coarse sea salt	½ teaspoon turmeric
2 teaspoons dried Mediterranean oregano or savory	2 tablespoons Harissa (page 83)
1 teaspoon dried rosemary	1 tablespoon Roasted Garlic
3 teaspoons caraway seed	and Pepper Paste (page 88)
1 teaspoon cumin seed	Olive oil

In a spice grinder, clean coffee grinder, or mortar, grind the salt, oregano or savory, rosemary, caraway, cumin, and turmeric to a fine powder. Transfer to a bowl and add the Harissa and Roasted Garlic and Pepper Paste. Add 2 or more teaspoons olive oil to make a thick paste. Transfer the rub to a small jar and top with olive oil to keep it from drying out.

North African Meat Rub will keep for up to 6 months in the refrigerator.

Makes about ½ cup.

Bharat

Olive oil scented with roses was listed on clay tablets dating from about the 13th century B.C., found in the palaces of Knossos. Although it is not clear if the ancient Greeks used that oil in foods or as a cosmetic, we do know that the Byzantines liked to add plenty of rose water along with garum, a fermented fish sauce, to their meat dishes. Today small, dried, fragrant rosebuds and rose water are used to flavor not only sweets but also the very spicy meat stews of some Mediterranean countries, especially in the Maghreb (Arab North Africa).

Use tablespoons of powdered *bharat* to flavor meat stews and stuffings.

3 dried rosebuds, stems discarded (see Mail-Order
   Sources, page 134)
1 tablespoon black peppercorns

1 cinnamon stick, 1 inch long
3 tablespoons coarse sea salt

Place the rosebuds, pepper, cinnamon stick, and salt in a spice grinder or clean coffee grinder and grind to a powder; keep in a well-sealed box. Or, to maintain the flavor of the spice mixture longer, crumble the rosebuds with your fingers, grind the peppercorns, chop the cinnamon stick coarsely, then toss everything together with the salt. Keep this mixture in an airtight container and grind to a powder just before using.

Bharat will keep for 2 to 3 months, unground.

Makes about ⅓ cup.

Pamperato

I FIRST LEARNED about this unusual Umbrian sweet Christmas bread from Carol Field's magnificent book *Celebrating Italy*. As Carol notes, the word *pamperato* means "peppered," and the mixture of honey, nuts, dried fruits, and pepper brings to mind Medieval sweet breads. I love it because it reminds me of the descriptions of ancient Greek flat sweet breads that I have found in the writings of Athenaeus and other classical authors.

In my version of Carol's original recipe, brandy is substituted for a few tablespoons of espresso coffee.

Pamperato is very rich. Serve it in small pieces with coffee or a dessert wine.

⅔ cup raisins

2–3 tablespoons brandy

1 cup walnuts, toasted

⅔ cup almonds, toasted

¼ cup pine nuts, toasted

3½ ounces semisweet chocolate, grated

½ cup chopped candied orange or tangerine peel

2 tablespoons honey

2 tablespoons water

¾ cup grape juice, reduced to ¼ cup, or ¼ cup red currant jelly

Grated nutmeg

Grated zest of 1 orange or tangerine

¼ teaspoon sea salt

6–10 grindings black pepper

1 cup unbleached all-purpose flour

Apricot jam, melted

Confectioners' sugar

Soak the raisins in the brandy and a little warm water for 30 minutes, then drain. Preheat the oven to 350°F.

Chop together the walnuts, almonds, and pine nuts. Mix the nuts with the raisins, chocolate, and candied citrus peel. Melt the honey in the 2 tablespoons water, then add to the fruit-nut mixture. Stir in the grape juice, nutmeg, zest, and salt and pepper. Reserve a little flour and mix the rest in, little by little, using a rubber spatula, until you have a dough that holds together. (Alternatively, if you want to use a food processor, place all the nuts, the grated chocolate, and the honey in the work bowl and, pulsing the motor on and off, chop until fine. Add the soaked raisins, candied orange peel, water, grape juice, nutmeg, orange zest, salt, pepper, and two-thirds of the flour. Process again, turning the motor on and off, until you have a sticky dough that holds together.)

Divide the dough into 3 balls. On a floured surface, shape each piece into a 5½-inch disk, incorporating the rest of the flour into the dough as you work.

Place the disks on a buttered and floured baking sheet and bake for 20 to 25 minutes, until firm. Brush the top of each disk with melted apricot jam and bake for another 5 minutes. Let cool briefly, then sprinkle confectioners' sugar through a sieve over the tops.

Store in an airtight tin. Let mellow for 2 to 3 days before serving.

Pamperato keeps for up to 1 month, improving as it ages.

Makes 3 *Pamperati*; serves 10 to 12.

Sweet Wine and Orange Rusks

THIS IS MY OWN variation of a sweet festive bread from Rethemnon, Crete.

1 cup sweet red wine, such as Greek Mavrodaphne

2 tablespoons honey

1 cinnamon stick, 2 inches long

1 tablespoon whole cloves

½ cup freshly squeezed orange juice

½ cup fine semolina

2½ cups unbleached all-purpose flour

1 tablespoon orange zest

½ teaspoon sea salt

2 packets active dry yeast, dissolved in ½ cup warm water

¼ cup olive oil, plus additional for brushing tops of loaves

Pour the wine into a small nonreactive saucepan. Add the honey, cinnamon stick, and cloves, and bring to a boil. Reduce the heat and let simmer for about 3 minutes, until you can smell the spices.

Remove from the heat, add the orange juice, and let the mixture cool slightly. Pass through a fine-meshed sieve into a bowl, then add the semolina, stirring constantly so lumps do not form.

In a large bowl, combine the flour with the orange zest and salt and mix thoroughly. Make a well in the center and pour in the yeast mixture, spiced wine, and olive oil.

(Continued on next page)

Draw the flour toward the center until all of it is mixed with the liquid. Start kneading the dough, sprinkling it with flour if it is too sticky or wetting your hands with warm water if it is too stiff. (Alternatively, if you want to use a food processor, place the flour, orange zest, and salt in the work bowl and, pulsing the motor on and off, process until mixed thoroughly. Add the yeast mixture, spiced wine, and olive oil. Process again, turning the motor on and off, until you have a sticky dough that holds together.)

When the dough becomes smooth and shiny, after about 10 to 15 minutes of kneading, shape into a ball, cover with plastic wrap, and let stand in a warm place for about 1½ to 2 hours, until doubled in size.

Roll out the dough on a floured surface, fold, and roll again a couple of times. Divide the dough into 3 pieces and shape each piece into a long sausage. Oil a baking sheet and place the loaves on it. Brush them with oil. With a sharp knife or razor blade, make shallow diagonal slashes on the surface of the breads at ½-inch intervals (as if you were starting to cut slices). Cover with plastic wrap and let stand for 45 minutes to 1 hour, until doubled in size.

Preheat the oven to 375°F. Bake the breads for 30 to 40 minutes, until golden brown. Turn upside down and bake for another 5 minutes, until they sound hollow when tapped with your fingers.

Let cool on a rack for 15 minutes.

Cut the bread into ½-inch slices. Turn down the oven to its lowest setting (175°F.).

Place the slices on the oven rack and bake for about 5 to 6 hours, until completely dry. Cool the slices on the oven rack and store in an airtight box.

The rusks will keep up to 6 months.

Makes about 45 to 50 rusks.

Rusks in Sweet Wine and Cinnamon

O<small>N THE ISLAND OF KEA</small>—where my mother grew up—when a family wants to notify friends and relatives that a memorial service will take place, a pan of these rusks, called *vrekto* in Greek, is taken around, and a piece is given to everyone who is invited to attend the ceremony.

These wine-dipped rusks make a simple and delicious dessert, plain or topped with ice cream or thick yogurt and orange preserves.

¼ cup sweet red wine, preferably Greek
   Mavrodaphne
8 Sweet Wine and Orange Rusks (page 47)
4 teaspoons sugar (optional)

1 teaspoon ground cinnamon, or to taste
Vanilla ice cream, or 1 cup thick yogurt
   and 8 slices Orange Slices in Syrup
   (page 121; optional)

In a bowl, combine the wine with 3 to 4 tablespoons of water. Dip the rusks in the liquid and turn to moisten on both sides. Sprinkle the rusks with the sugar and cinnamon. Place 2 rusks on each of 4 plates and top with the ice cream or yogurt. Garnish with the orange preserves.

Serves 4.

Honey Cookies

THESE DELICIOUS GREEK COOKIES, flavored with thyme-scented honey, orange juice and zest, brandy, cinnamon, and cloves, are traditionally prepared for Christmas. The recipe is my mother's, passed to her from her mother. The deep flavor of these cookies, called *melomakarona* in Greek, actually improves with time.

Serve after dinner with coffee and sweet wine.

1¼ cups light olive oil (or half olive oil and half canola or safflower oil)

⅓ cup sugar

1 cup freshly squeezed orange juice

3–4 cups unbleached all-purpose flour

2½ teaspoons baking powder

½ cup brandy

1½ cups fine semolina

Grated zest of 1 orange

Grated zest of 1 lemon

1 teaspoon ground cloves

½ teaspoon ground cinnamon

FOR THE HONEY SYRUP

1 cup sugar

1 cup honey

2 cups water

A large piece of orange peel

A large piece of lemon peel

1 cup coarsely ground walnuts

2 teaspoons ground cloves

Using an electric mixer, beat the olive oil with the sugar in a large bowl. Add the orange juice. In a separate bowl, mix 2 cups of the flour with the baking powder. Gradually beat the flour mixture into the oil and orange juice mixture. Beat in the brandy, semolina, orange and lemon peels, cloves, and cinnamon.

Turn the mixture out onto a floured surface and start kneading, adding more flour as necessary, until you obtain a soft and elastic dough. Cover the dough with plastic wrap and let it rest for about 25 minutes.

Preheat the oven to 350°F.

Break off tablespoons of dough, roll them in your hands, then shape them into oval cookies about 2 inches long. Press the tines of a fork lightly on the top of each cookie to make a decorative pattern. Place them on a baking sheet and bake for about 20 to 25 minutes, until light brown. Let them cool on a rack.

The next day, make the honey syrup. In a saucepan, combine the sugar, honey, and water, and bring to a boil. Add the orange and lemon peels and simmer for 5 to 10 minutes to let the flavors blend. Turn the heat to low to keep the syrup liquid. Place 2 or 3 cookies on a large slotted spoon and dip them into the syrup. Don't let them soak in it—they should absorb only a little syrup and remain crunchy.

Place 1 layer of honey-dipped *melomakarona* on a dish. Combine the walnuts with the ground cloves, then sprinkle the mixture over the cookies. Repeat with all of the cookies.

Let the cookies cool completely before serving.

Honey Cookies keep well for 3 to 4 weeks, stored in an airtight container.

Makes 60 to 70 cookies.

OVERLEAF
Roasted Almond Cookies, Dried Fig and Apricot Balls, Honey Cookies, and Pamperato

Roasted Almond Cookies

Greeks call these delicate cookies, which melt in your mouth, *kourambiedes*. They are coated with confectioners' sugar and traditionally prepared every Christmas.

The old recipe uses olive oil, as all Greek sweets did before the country was conquered by the Ottomans in the 15th century. The use of butter then became increasingly common, and *kourambiedes* as well as many other sweets are prepared today almost exclusively with butter. But even cooks who choose to make their holiday *kourambiedes* with butter sometimes make them with olive oil during Lent, when religious practice forbids all foods that contain animal products, and there are some regional cooks, in the Peloponnese and in the North, who prefer the original recipe, a variation of which I present here.

½ cup olive oil

½ cup sunflower oil

⅓ cup confectioners' sugar, plus about 2 cups
   to sprinkle on the cookies

1 egg yolk

Zest of 1 lemon

3 tablespoons ouzo, pastis, or any
   other anise-flavored liqueur

3 cups unbleached all-purpose flour

1 teaspoon baking powder

1 cup coarsely ground toasted almonds

In a food processor or electric mixer, process the olive and sunflower oils with ⅓ cup confectioners' sugar for about 8 to 10 minutes. Add the egg yolk, lemon zest, and ouzo and process for 3 to 4 minutes more. Sift the flour with the baking powder. Pour the liquids out of the food processor and then fit the processor with a dough hook. Add liquids again, and gradually add the flour. Process the mixture for 3 to 5 minutes, until a soft dough forms. Add the almonds and process until the dough is smooth again, about 3 minutes more.

Preheat the oven to 350°F.

Shape tablespoons of dough into round, oval, or crescent-shaped cookies and place on a cookie sheet, leaving about 1 inch between the cookies so that they won't stick together as they expand. Bake for 20 to 25 minutes, until a very pale golden. Cool for 5 minutes. Spread 1 cup confectioners' sugar on a very large serving plate. Very carefully, because they break easily, roll a cookie in the sugar, and place on a rack to cool. Proceed with all the cookies, adding more sugar to the plate as necessary. Finally, sift additional sugar on top of the cookies and let rest for 3 to 4 hours or overnight.

Carefully pack the cookies in boxes, spreading a piece of waxed paper between each layer.

Roasted Almond Cookies will keep for 2 months or longer.

Makes 36 cookies.

NOTE: Instead of roasted almonds, some cooks prefer to use raw almonds without removing their skins, especially if they have a source for excellent-quality fresh nuts.

Yogurt, Lemon, and Pistachio Biscotti

Yogurt cake is one of the most common Greek desserts. The basic recipe, in which yogurt is the only source of fat, probably originated in Turkey, where similar cakes are also common. Almonds, walnuts, pistachios, mastic, vanilla, cinnamon, and lemon or orange zest are some of the flavorings used to enrich the basic recipe. The cakes are often made even richer with a sugar or honey syrup, or are sliced and baked again in a slow oven to become *biscotti* (called *biskota* in Greek). These very tasty biscuits are quite hard. Serve with coffee, tea, or sweet wine.

1 cup fine semolina flour

1 cup unbleached all-purpose flour

1 cup sugar

Zest of 1 lemon

1 tablespoon baking powder

3 tablespoons brandy

1½ cups thick sheep's milk yogurt (see Note)

3 eggs

1 cup blanched and peeled pistachio nuts

Preheat the oven to 375°F. Grease a 12-x-9-x-2-inch baking pan.

Place the semolina and all-purpose flours, sugar, and lemon zest in the bowl of a food processor. Combine the baking powder and brandy, then add the mixture to the processor bowl along with the yogurt and eggs. Process for 30 seconds to 1 minute, until you obtain a very smooth batter. Pour the batter into a clean bowl and stir in the pistachios. Transfer the batter to the prepared baking pan and bake for about 30 minutes, or until a toothpick inserted in the center comes out clean.

Let the cake cool and turn the oven to its lowest setting (about 175° to 200°F.). Invert the cooled cake onto a wooden board. With a very sharp knife, cut the cake from short side to short side into 4 long strips. Slice each strip into ½-inch-wide rectangles and place on an oven rack, overlapping slightly. Bake again for about 2 hours, until completely dry. Let cool on the rack before packing in airtight boxes.

Yogurt, Lemon, and Pistachio Biscotti will keep for up to six months if packed airtight. Makes about 75 *biscotti*.

NOTE: If you cannot find sheep's milk yogurt (see Mail-Order Sources, page 134), drain ordinary cow's milk yogurt in a sieve lined with cheesecloth for about 30 minutes, then add ½ cup heavy cream to the recipe.

VARIATION: To make Orange and Almond Biscotti, substitute orange zest for the lemon zest and almonds for the pistachios.

Greek Easter Bread Biscotti

GREEK EASTER BREAD (*tsourecki*) is very similar to Italian *panetone,* but it contains less fat and more spices. In many Athenian bakeries Greek *tsourecki* is sliced and baked again to make these *biscotti.* Unlike *biscotti* prepared with yogurt, these are extremely light and absorb liquids immediately.

Serve with coffee or tea or use as a base for English trifle or bread puddings.

¼ cup warm milk plus 2 tablespoons cold milk for brushing on loaves

2 tablespoons honey

1½ tablespoons active dry yeast

¼ cup unsalted butter or margarine

¼ cup sugar

2 tablespoons olive oil

¼ cup orange juice

1 teaspoon ground mastic (see Mail-Order Sources, page 134)

1 teaspoon ground mahlep (see Mail-Order Sources, page 134)

3 tablespoons grated orange rind

3 eggs, separated

4–5 cups unbleached all-purpose flour

½ teaspoon salt

In a small bowl, combine the warm milk and 1 tablespoon of the honey. Add the yeast and leave to dissolve.

In another bowl, beat the butter with the sugar and remaining honey. Add the olive oil, orange juice, mastic, mahlep, and grated orange rind. Continue beating while adding the eggs, one by one, reserving ½ egg yolk.

Sift 4 cups of the flour with the salt and make a well in the center. Pour in the yeast and the butter mixtures and stir to form a dough. Knead with your hands for about 10 minutes, adding a little more flour if the dough is too sticky or warm milk if it is too hard. (Alternatively, work the dough in a food processor or electric mixer fitted with the dough hook.)

When the dough becomes soft and shiny, form it into a ball, place it in an oiled bowl, cover, and let rise for about 2 hours, until doubled in size.

When doubled in size, punch the dough down and divide it into 3 equal pieces. Roll each piece into a loaf about 15 inches long. Place the loaves on a buttered baking pan and cover. Let rise for another 2 to 3 hours, until doubled in size.

Preheat the oven to 375°F.

Beat the remaining ½ egg yolk with 2 tablespoons milk and brush the mixture on the loaves. Bake for 30 to 40 minutes, until nicely browned. Let cool on a rack. Cut the loaves into ½-inch slices and place the slices on the rack of a just-warm (175° to 200°F.) oven for about 2 to 3 hours, until dry.

Pack in airtight boxes.

Greek Easter Bread Biscotti will keep for up to six months if packed airtight.

Makes about 85 *biscotti*.

Cretan Barley Paximadia

ALTHOUGH MOST *paximadia* become very hard when they are dried, these are quite crunchy. For a first course or light lunch, top them with chopped fresh tomato, onions, bell pepper, and a little fresh chili pepper. Then sprinkle with dried oregano, drizzle with extra-virgin olive oil, and serve with feta cheese.

Cretan Barley Paximadia are also the ideal accompaniment to cheese and all kinds of spreads, including the Arugula and Parsley Spread that you will find on page 61.

2 tablespoons honey

Approximately 1⅓ cups warm water, or more if needed

2 tablespoons active dry yeast (preferably Saf-Instant; see Mail-Order Sources, page 134)

1 tablespoon coarse sea salt

1 tablespoon green aniseed or star anise

2–2½ cups unbleached all-purpose flour

2 cups whole barley flour

½ cup olive oil

½ cup sweet red wine, such as Greek Mavrodaphne or port

½ cup dry red wine

Olive oil, for brushing on the dough and baking sheets

In a 4-cup bowl, dilute the honey with ⅓ cup of the warm water. Add the yeast, stir, and leave to proof for 10 minutes.

In a mortar, pound the salt with the aniseed until you get a coarse powder. In a large bowl, stir together the all-purpose and whole barley flours and the aniseed-salt powder. Make a well in the center and pour in the olive oil, the sweet and dry red wines, the yeast mixture, and ½ cup warm water. Draw the flour towards the center, mixing it with the liquids to form a rather sticky dough. Knead patiently, adding a little more warm water or flour to obtain a smooth dough.

(Alternatively, make this dough in a food processor or electric mixer equipped with dough hooks. Add all ingredients to the work bowl and process for 3 minutes at high speed. Scrape the bowl with a spatula, let rest for 5 to 10 minutes, then process another 3 minutes.)

Turn the dough out onto a lightly floured board and continue kneading, folding, pushing, turning, and folding for another 2 to 3 minutes. You must end up with a soft, very slightly sticky dough. Form a ball, oil it all over with a few drops of olive oil, place in a 3-quart bowl, cover with plastic wrap, and let rise in a draft-free place for about 1½ hours, until it has doubled in size.

Cut the dough in half and divide each piece into quarters. Form each piece into a 1-inch-thick cord, then shape each cord into a small circle with overlapping ends (see photograph on page 60). Place the circles on lightly oiled baking sheets, spaced 1½ inches apart. Cover with plastic wrap and let rise for about 2 more hours.

Preheat the oven to 400°F.

When you place the bread circles in the oven, reduce the temperature to 375°F. Bake for 30 to 40 minutes, until the bread circles are light golden on top and sound hollow when tapped.

Let them cool for 5 to 10 minutes. Turn the oven down to its lowest setting (175°F.). Using a very good bread knife, slice the circles in half horizontally. Place the halves on the oven rack and leave for about 1½ to 2 hours, until they are completely dry. Let cool and keep in tins in a dry place.

Cretan Barley Paximadia will keep for up to 6 months.

Makes 16 large (4½-inch) biscuits.

Arugula and Parsley Spread

M<small>Y FRIEND FENY XYDI</small>, a very imaginative cook, gave me this simple, light, and very tasty recipe. I cannot decide whether I like it better with scallions or with garlic, so I give you both options.

Serve with crudités and Cretan Barley Paximadia (page 58) or Olive Oil, Pepper, and Ouzo Biscuits (page 63).

1 Cretan Barley Paximadia (page 58)

1 cup coarsely chopped arugula

2 cups coarsely chopped flat-leaf parsley

2–3 scallions or 1 small garlic clove, cut lengthwise and sprout removed

3–5 tablespoons extra-virgin olive oil

3–4 tablespoons fresh lemon juice

Sea salt and freshly ground black pepper, to taste

OPPOSITE

Olive Oil, Ouzo, and Pepper Biscuits, Saffron Biscuits, and Cretan Barley Paximadia

Soak the biscuit in water for 5 to 10 minutes, until soft. Squeeze the biscuits with your hands to remove most of the water. Drop in the bowl of a blender or food processor. Add the arugula, parsley, scallions or garlic, olive oil, and 3 tablespoons lemon juice. Process until you obtain a smooth paste. Taste and adjust the seasoning, adding salt, pepper, and more lemon juice if needed. Refrigerate for 2 to 3 hours before serving.

Makes about 2 cups.

Saffron Biscuits

MODERN GREEKS very rarely use saffron in their cooking or baking, but yellow saffron biscuits are prepared every Easter on the island of Astypalaia. The traditional Astypalaian method of preparing these biscuits is somewhat complicated, so I have created the following simplified version.

Serve Saffron Biscuits by themselves or with fresh cheese such as ricotta or Greek Manouri.

2 tablespoons honey, preferably thyme-scented

Approximately ⅔ cup warm water

1½ tablespoons active dry yeast (preferably Saf-Instant; see Mail-Order Sources, page 134)

1 cup milk

⅔ teaspoon saffron threads (see Mail-Order Sources, page 134)

3½–4 cups unbleached all-purpose flour

½–1 teaspoon ground white pepper, or to taste

½ teaspoon ground allspice

1 tablespoon sea salt

½ cup virgin olive oil

In a small bowl, dissolve the honey in ⅓ cup warm water. Stir in the yeast and leave to proof for about 10 minutes.

In a small saucepan, warm ½ cup of milk with the saffron threads. Simmer for about 3 minutes. Let cool, add the remaining milk, and measure. You should have about ⅔ cup.

Sift 3½ cups flour into a large bowl, then stir in the pepper, allspice, and salt. Make a well in the center of the flour and pour in the yeast mixture, saffron milk, olive oil, and ⅓ cup warm water. Start drawing flour towards the center and mixing it with the liquids to form a dough. Knead very well for about 15 minutes, until you obtain a soft, smooth dough. Add a little more flour or water if needed.

(Alternatively, when the yeast mixture is ready, place the flour and all of the other ingredients in a bowl of a food processor or mixer equipped with dough hooks, and process for about 3 minutes. Let rest for 10 minutes, then process for another 3 minutes.)

Turn the smooth dough out onto a lightly floured board and knead it for about 3 more minutes, folding, pushing, and turning. Shape the dough into a ball, then brush with a little olive oil, cover with plastic wrap, and let rise in a draft-free place for about 2 hours, until doubled in size.

Turn the dough out onto a lightly floured board. Punch the dough a few times, then flatten it well with your hands, fold it, and punch again. Divide the dough into quarters and form each piece into a 1-inch-thick, 15-inch-long baguette. Place on a baking sheet, cover again with plastic wrap, and let rise for 1½ to 2 hours, until doubled in size.

Preheat the oven to 375°F.

Bake the loaves for 25 to 30 minutes, until they are lightly golden and sound hollow when tapped. Cool on a rack for about 10 minutes.

With a good bread knife, cut the baguettes into ½-inch slices. Place the slices on the rack of an oven set on its lowest setting (175°F.) and leave them to dry completely, about 1 ½ to 2 hours. Cool the biscuits on a rack and pack in boxes.

Saffron Biscuits will keep for up to 6 months.

Makes about 60 biscuits.

Olive Oil, Pepper, and Ouzo Biscuits

SERVE OLIVE OIL, PEPPER, AND OUZO BISCUITS by themselves as snacks or to accompany cheese or any savory spread as appetizers.

2 tablespoons honey, preferably thyme-scented

Approximately 1 cup warm water

1½ tablespoons active dry yeast (preferably Saf-Instant; see Mail-Order Sources, page 134)

3½–4 cups unbleached all-purpose flour

1½ tablespoons coarsely ground black pepper

1 tablespoon ground aniseed

1 tablespoon sea salt

1 tablespoon sea salt

⅓ cup ouzo or any other anise-flavored liqueur

½ cup virgin olive oil, plus additional for brushing dough

2–3 tablespoons nigella (optional; see Mail-Order Sources, page 134)

In a small bowl, dissolve the honey in ⅓ cup warm water. Stir in the yeast and leave to proof for 10 minutes. Sift 3½ cups flour into a large bowl. Stir in the pepper, aniseed, and salt.

Make a well in the center of the flour and pour in the yeast mixture, ouzo, olive oil, and the remaining ½ cup warm water. Draw the flour towards the center and mix it with the liquids to form a dough. Knead very well for about 15 minutes, until you obtain a soft, smooth dough. Add a little more flour or water if needed.

(Alternatively, when the yeast mixture is ready, place the flour and all of the other ingredients in the bowl of a food processor or a mixer equipped with dough hooks, and process the mixture for about 3 minutes.)

Turn the smooth dough out onto a lightly floured board, knead it a bit more, and shape it into a ball. Brush with a little olive oil, cover with plastic wrap, and let rise in a draft-free place for 2 hours, until doubled in size.

Turn the dough out onto a lightly floured board, punch a few times, flatten it well with your hands, then fold it and punch again.

(Continued on next page)

Divide the dough into quarters and shape each piece into a 1-inch-thick, 15-inch-long baguette. If you like, sprinkle with nigella. Place on a baking sheet, cover again with plastic wrap, and let rise for 1 to 2 hours, until doubled in size.

Preheat the oven to 375°F.

Bake the loaves for 25 to 30 minutes, until they are golden brown and sound hollow when tapped. Cool on a rack for 15 to 25 minutes.

With a good bread knife, cut the baguettes into ½-inch slices. Place the slices on the rack of an oven set at its lowest setting (175°F.) and leave them to dry completely, about 3 hours. Cool on a rack and pack in boxes.

Olive Oil, Pepper, and Ouzo Biscuits will keep for up to 6 months.

Makes about 65 biscuits.

VARIATION: To make Mastic Biscuits, substitute a flavorless spirit such as vodka for the ouzo, and substitute mastic (see Mail-Order Sources, page 134) for the aniseed. Mix the mastic with the salt and pound in a stone or porcelain mortar to grind.

Mediterranean bread seasoning can be used to add extra flavor to any kind of bread, such as white, whole wheat, or multi-grain. Use 1 tablespoon for each 4 cups flour in the recipe. (Add extra salt only if your recipe calls for more than 1 teaspoon per 4 cups flour.)

    7 tablespoons mastic (see Mail-Order Sources, page 134)
    10 tablespoons coarse sea salt
    8 tablespoons mahlep seed (see Mail-Order Sources, page 134)

To grind the mastic, mix the dry resin with 2 to 3 tablespoons of the salt and grind in a stone or porcelain mortar.

Grind the mahlep in a spice grinder, coffee grinder, or mortar with the rest of the salt. Thoroughly combine the mastic, mahlep, and salt. Store in an airtight box in a dry place.

Mediterranean Bread Seasoning will keep for 3 to 4 months.

Makes about 1 cup.

VARIATION: If you want a bread that tastes like licorice, substitute green aniseed or star anise for the mastic.

Dried Apple Peels

Wild aromatic herbs, flower petals, tree leaves, dried fruits, and fruit peels and stems make the most delicious tisanes. Many are consumed for medicinal purposes—an ancient tradition in the Mediterranean—while others are consumed for pleasure because people like their taste and aroma.

In Greece we love sage, lime blossom (*tilleul*), and mountain tea (*Sideritis theezans*). The Spaniards love *herba louisa* (lemon verbena). In Tunisia, herbal tea made from dried mint is served with a few pine nuts floating on the surface.

In Turkey, the most favored tisane, traditionally served in small tulip-shaped glasses, is made by boiling apple peels in water. Tourists who visit the charming Egyptian Bazaar—the spice market in Istanbul—always come home with bags full of dried apple peels. If you can't make it to Istanbul to buy a supply, try this recipe.

Peels of 10–12 apples

Place the peels on a rack in a warm oven (175° to 200°F.) and let dry for about 4 hours, or overnight.

Let cool, then pack in an airtight box and store in a dry place.

Dried Apple Peels will keep for up to a year if properly dried and stored.

Makes enough peels for about 12 cups of tea.

Apple Peel Tea

Apple peel tea, which is delicious hot, can be served cold, with ice cubes. If you like, you can decorate each glass with a sprig of fresh mint, which gives the apple peels a fresher and more fragrant taste.

1 quart water

Dried peels of 4 apples (see page 66)

½ cinnamon stick, 1 inch long

3 whole cloves

Sugar or honey (optional)

Bring the water to a boil. Add the apple peels and simmer for about 4 minutes. Add the spices and simmer 30 seconds more. Remove from the heat and let stand for 1 minute.

Strain through a sieve and serve with sugar or honey on the side, if desired.

Serves 4.

Mashed dried figs, mixed with honey and nuts, was one of the desserts ancient Greeks liked to eat while sipping their strong, sweet wines. In a similar vein, the Arabs have always loved their *hais,* a simple sweet made by kneading together chopped pitted dates and walnuts, pistachios, bread crumbs, and a little sesame oil. *Haroset* (or *charozeth*), the traditional fruit and nut mixture that is served at the Jewish Passover, is a similar concoction.

My variation on this theme is a combination of dried fruits, nuts, honey, and a little sweet wine. I'm sure you will love these little fruity balls that were inspired by the first sweets cooks ever created.

Serve after lunch or dinner, with coffee or tea.

1 cup blanched and peeled almonds

1 cup walnuts

12 dried figs

24 good-quality dried apricots (see recipe introduction on page 115)

½ teaspoon ground nutmeg

⅔ teaspoon ground cinnamon

3 tablespoons honey, preferably thyme-scented

2–4 tablespoons or more sweet white wine, preferably Samos Vin de Liqueur

40 bay leaves, fresh or dried

Place the almonds, walnuts, figs, and apricots in the bowl of a food processor. Add the nutmeg, cinnamon, honey, and 2 tablespoons of the wine. Process, pulsing to start and then letting the motor run continuously, until you have an homogeneous sticky dough. If it is too hard, add a little more wine to facilitate the process.

One tablespoon at a time, shape the dough into a ball by rolling it between your palms. Scrape your hands with a spatula when they become too sticky to continue.

Place each ball on a bay leaf, and let sit, uncovered, for 4 to 5 hours or overnight. Pack with the bay leaves in boxes and keep in a dry, cool place.

Dried Fig and Apricot Balls will keep for about 2 months.

Makes about 50.

Dried Artichokes and Leeks

DRYING ARTICHOKES involves quite a bit of work, but they are so tasty that I think it is worth the effort. If you dry leeks at the same time, you will be ready to prepare a delicious risotto in minutes (see following page). Or you can easily pull together a pasta sauce by soaking the artichokes and leeks in water; sautéing them with garlic, chili pepper, and olive oil; then adding cream or some concentrated chicken stock.

Juice of 2 medium lemons plus 1 large lemon
8 artichokes, about 2½ inches in diameter
8 leeks, white part only

Pour about 1 quart water into a bowl and add the lemon juice.

Remove the outer hard leaves of an artichoke with a sharp knife and keep snapping off leaves until you are left with a soft cone formed by the inner leaves and the heart.

Cut the large lemon in half and rub the artichoke to prevent discoloration. Trim the green top of the cone and halve the artichoke. Rub with lemon and, with a teaspoon, remove the hairy choke. After rubbing again with lemon, place the artichoke pieces in the bowl of lemon water while preparing the rest of the artichokes.

Cut each artichoke half into quarters lengthwise, rubbing each piece with the lemon, and place on the rack of a very slow (175° to 200°F.) oven. If any of the artichokes have long stems, peel off and discard the stringy outer layer, cut the stem in half lengthwise, rub with lemon, and dry together with the other artichoke pieces.

Halve each leek lengthwise, then cut each half into pieces measuring about 1 inch. Wash well, drain on paper towels, and arrange on a piece of thin wire mesh or on a piece of cheesecloth placed on an oven rack. Place the leeks in the oven with the artichokes.

Leave the artichokes and leeks in the oven for about 4 hours, or overnight, until completely dry. Let cool, then break with your fingers and mix the pieces together. Store in airtight boxes.

Properly dried artichokes and leeks will keep for more than a year.

Makes about 4 cups.

NOTE: Even though the artichokes are rubbed with lemon, they will turn dark as they dry. This is natural—it happens with most green vegetables and doesn't alter their taste. Unfortunately, only chemically treated vegetables and fruits remain light-colored when dried.

Artichoke and Leek Risotto

1½ cups Dried Artichokes and Leeks (previous page), soaked in 2 cups warm water for about 4 hours

1½–2 cups chicken stock (see Mail-Order Sources, page 134)

3–4 tablespoons olive oil

2–3 garlic cloves, minced

⅓–½ chili pepper, chopped; or ⅓–½ teaspoon Near Eastern or Aleppo crushed red pepper (see Mail-Order Sources, page 134)

1½ cups Arborio rice

¼ cup pitted chopped green olives, preferably Greek cracked olives, soaked in water and rinsed

½ cup dry white wine

3–4 tablespoons fresh lemon juice

½ cup chopped dill

Salt and freshly ground black pepper to taste

½–1 cup grated Parmesan cheese

Drain the artichokes and leeks, reserving the liquid. Combine the chicken stock and soaking liquid in a medium saucepan and bring to a simmer.

Sauté the soaked vegetables in the olive oil in a nonreactive saucepan for 1 minute. Add the garlic and chili pepper and sauté for 30 seconds, then add the rice and turn with a wooden spoon to coat with the oil. Add the olives and pour in the wine and a little of the stock. Cook, stirring constantly and adding more stock as the rice absorbs it, until the rice is cooked through but not mushy, about 20 minutes.

Stir in the lemon juice and dill, taste, and adjust the seasoning with salt and pepper. Sprinkle with the Parmesan and serve at once.

Serves 4 as a main course.

Frankincense—the resin from trees of the genus *Boswellia* or from the eponymous fir—was one of the gifts given to the infant Christ by the Magi, and was also the favorite incense of ancient Greeks and Romans. Today frankincense is used mainly in religious ceremonies, but burning herbs and gums to fill houses and public spaces with sweet smells is still very common around the Mediterranean.

My grandmother used to burn a combination of lavender, rosemary, and thyme in a special cast-iron incense burner. I still remember the smell, which reminded me of mountain air in the summer. Use only the best-quality, most fragrant herbs for this mixture.

5 tablespoons dried lavender

4 tablespoons dried rosemary

3 tablespoons dried thyme

3 tablespoons dried oregano

5 dried bay leaves, crumbled

Toss all the ingredients very well with your fingers.

Keep in an airtight box and burn teaspoonfuls on small, specially treated charcoal tablets (see Mail-Order Sources, page 134). Alternatively, add the herbs to wax when making candles.

Mixed Herb Incense will keep for about 6 months.

Makes about 1 cup.

IN JARS

Olive and Herb Spread

Tapenade, the famous olive, caper, and anchovy spread prepared in the South of France, has its roots in antiquity. The Roman statesman Cato (234–149 B.C.) describes a preparation that combined pitted and chopped black, green, and mottled olives with coriander, fennel, cumin, rue, mint, olive oil, and vinegar. My olive spread is inspired by this ancient recipe.

Make Olive and Herb Spread at least one day in advance of serving to give the flavors a chance to meld. Serve with toasted bread, as an appetizer.

1½ cups juicy black olives

1½ cups cracked green olives

3 tablespoons chopped fresh coriander

½ cup chopped fresh wild fennel or fennel tops

2 garlic cloves

3 tablespoons chopped fresh mint leaves

½–1 teaspoon Green Chili Pepper Paste (page 87)
  or freshly ground white pepper to taste

1½ tablespoons red wine vinegar

1–2 tablespoons balsamic vinegar,
  or to taste

4 tablespoons extra-virgin olive oil

Virgin olive oil, to top the jar

Rinse the olives thoroughly in running water. Taste them, and if they are still very salty, let them stand for 1 to 2 hours in warm water before rinsing again. Dry on paper towels. Remove the pits and chop coarsely.

Place the olives, coriander, fennel, garlic, mint, chili pepper paste, red wine vinegar, and 1 tablespoon of the balsamic vinegar in a food processor. Process until you obtain a homogeneous paste, then, with the motor running, slowly add the extra-virgin olive oil. Taste and adjust the seasoning, adding a little white pepper or more vinegar if needed.

Transfer the olive paste to a jar, top with a little virgin olive oil so that the paste is completely covered, cover the jar, and place in the refrigerator for at least 1 day before serving.

This olive spread will keep for up to 1 month in the refrigerator.

Makes about 2 cups.

Eggplant, Pepper, and Walnut Spread

Serve this spread as an appetizer, with crudités or with Cretan Barley Paximadia (see page 58) or Olive Oil, Pepper, and Ouzo Biscuits (see page 63). It is also good on baked or steamed potatoes.

2 large eggplants (about 2 pounds)

3 tablespoons olive oil

½–1 teaspoon Near Eastern or Aleppo crushed red pepper (see Mail-Order Sources, page 134) or red pepper flakes

3 green bell peppers, seeded, halved, and cut into ½-inch pieces

1 large garlic clove

1 cup walnuts

2 teaspoons sherry vinegar, or to taste

2 tablespoons extra-virgin olive oil, plus extra for topping the jars

½ teaspoon sea salt, or to taste

Wash and dry the eggplants. Preheat the broiler. To develop a smoky flavor, broil the whole eggplants, turning occasionally, until the skins blacken on all sides, about 40 minutes total. (Alternatively, place 3 layers of aluminum foil on an electric burner, place the eggplants on the foil, and sear, letting the skin blacken on one side before turning to blacken on another side, about 35 minutes total.)

When they are cool enough to handle, peel the eggplants and discard any seeds. Let the pulp drain in a colander for at least 30 minutes.

Meanwhile, warm the 3 tablespoons olive oil in a skillet. Add the crushed red pepper and the bell peppers and sauté until the peppers are soft, about 6 to 10 minutes. Let cool.

Cut the garlic clove lengthwise and discard the green sprout.

Place the drained eggplant pulp, the fried peppers with their oil, walnuts, vinegar, extra-virgin olive oil, and salt in the bowl of a food processor. Process, pulsing the motor on and off, until the mixture becomes a smooth spread. Taste and add more salt or vinegar if needed.

Place the spread in jars, pressing down on it to eliminate all air pockets. Top each jar with a little olive oil and refrigerate.

Eggplant, Pepper, and Walnut Spread will keep for 3 to 4 weeks.

Makes about 3½ cups.

Whereas westerners tend to use only the juice of the lemon, North Africans preserve whole lemons in a brine made with their juice and coarse sea salt (as in this recipe), then eat the skin and white pith. Following the North African tradition, use chopped Preserved Lemons to season salads, steamed potatoes, or other vegetables (see Tunisian Carrot Salad, page 85). It is also a particularly tasty addition to chicken baked with lots of garlic.

4–5 large, thick-skinned lemons

⅔–1 cup coarse sea salt

1 tablespoon pink peppercorns

1 cinnamon stick, 2 inches long

2 bay leaves

1–1½ cups lemon juice

Olive oil

Wash and dry the lemons. Cut them in quarters or eighths without detaching the pieces completely at the stem end. In a bowl, toss the lemons with the salt, pressing down on the lemons to extract most of their juice.

Place the salt-coated lemons in a 1½-quart jar. Add the pink peppercorns, cinnamon stick, and bay leaves, and fill the jar with enough lemon juice to cover the lemons completely. You may need to add a little more lemon juice and salt to fill the jar. Cover and keep in a cool, dry place for 2 weeks, shaking the jar every day.

To store, top with a little olive oil and keep in the refrigerator. To use, discard the juicy flesh, wash the pith and skin under cold water, and chop.

Preserved lemons will keep up to 6 months. They become very sour after that.

Makes 1½ quarts.

NOTE: To get rid of the bitter taste of the skin, some people like to soak the lemons in cold water, changed daily, for 2 to 3 days before preserving. I find that this diminishes the pungent flavor and aroma of the preserved lemons.

Lemon Slices in Olive Oil

THIS IS AN ALGERIAN variation of the preserved lemons found throughout North Africa. Use chopped skin and pith in salads and meat and poultry stews (also see uses of Preserved Lemons on the preceding page). The fragrant olive oil from these preserves can be added in very small amounts to salad dressings and marinades.

> 3–4 lemons
> 4–6 tablespoons sea salt
> Approximately 1 cup virgin olive oil

Wash and dry the lemons thoroughly. Cut them into ⅛-inch slices and lay 1 layer in a stainless steel colander. Sprinkle the lemon slices with plenty of salt and repeat until you have used all the lemons and salt. Set aside to drain for 24 hours.

Press the lemon slices carefully to extract most of the juice, then pack the slices in a pint jar. Completely cover the lemon slices with olive oil.

The lemon slices will keep in the refrigerator for 3 to 6 months.

Makes 2 cups.

Sweet-and-Sour Dried Figs

Sweet-and-sour fruits are made in Provence with fresh seedless grapes, peaches, pears, and other fruits. Dried figs are particularly suitable for this treatment, as are prunes and dried apricots. The bay leaves give this dish a Greek touch, because Greeks always use bay leaves when they cook figs.

Serve with thinly sliced prosciutto, other cured meats and game, or with grilled poultry, especially duck.

¾ pound dried figs

1 tablespoon whole cloves

2 bay leaves

1 small dried mild chili pepper (optional)

1 cinnamon stick, 1 inch long

Approximately 1 cup sherry vinegar or other good-quality wine vinegar

2–3 tablespoons honey

Pack the figs in a sterilized 1-pint glass jar. Add the cloves, bay leaves, chili pepper, and cinnamon stick. In a nonreactive saucepan, warm the vinegar with the honey and stir until the honey dissolves, being careful not to let the mixture boil. Pour the warm vinegar-honey mixture over the figs, topping with a little more vinegar if needed to cover them completely. Close the jar and leave in a cool place for at least 1 week before using, shaking from time to time.

Sweet-and-Sour Dried Figs will keep for a year or more. As you consume them, you can add more figs to the honey-vinegar mixture in the jar.

Makes 2 cups.

VARIATION: Substitute dried apricots or peaches for the figs.

Sweet-and-Sour Cherries

I FIRST CAME ACROSS a recipe for sweet-and-sour cherries many years ago in one of Elizabeth David's extraordinary books, and I have been making them regularly ever since. It is unusual for Greeks to eat cherries as a savory appetizer—we make only sweet preserves, syrups, and drinks with cherries—but in France and other parts of the Mediterranean, eating all kinds of savory sweet-and-sour fruits is very common. The following is my version of Elizabeth David's basic recipe.

Serve Sweet-and-Sour Cherries as you would olives, or pit them and add to salads or to sauces for poultry or game. Their spiced vinegar gives extra zing to salad dressings.

2 pounds firm, fresh sour cherries, such as Morellos, or a mixture of 2 or 3 cherry varieties	1 teaspoon white peppercorns
2½–3 cups white wine vinegar	2 cinnamon sticks, each 1 inch long
2 cups sugar	2 whole allspice berries
	1 teaspoon whole cloves

Wash and dry the cherries. Clip their stems to about 1 inch.

In a nonreactive pan, warm 2½ cups of the vinegar with the sugar, peppercorns, cinnamon sticks, allspice, and cloves.

Pack the cherries in 2 sterilized 1-quart jars and pour the spiced vinegar over them. Be careful to divide the spices equally between the 2 jars. Add a little more vinegar if necessary to cover the fruit completely. Cover and let stand at room temperature for about 3 to 4 weeks before consuming.

Sweet-and-Sour Cherries will keep for a year or more.

Makes 2 quarts.

I FIRST LEARNED about this marvelous hot chili pepper paste from food writer Paula Wolfert, who knows more about North African and Mediterranean cooking than anyone else. She extolled the virtues of homemade Tunisian *harissa,* and when I tried it during a visit to Tunisia, I became addicted immediately. It is incredible how just a small amount gives great depth of flavor to salads, sauces, stews, and dressings. I also like to mix a little *harissa* with a fruity olive oil and place it on the dinner table in a small bowl for bread-dipping.

Following is a variation of Paula's basic recipe.

⅓ cup (1½ ounces) Near Eastern or Aleppo crushed red pepper (see Mail-Order Sources, page 134), or 8 dried New Mexican chili peppers (see Mail-Order Sources, page 134), or ⅓ cup red pepper flakes mixed with 1 tablespoon paprika (see Note)

1 teaspoon Roasted Garlic and Pepper Paste (page 88) or 1 garlic clove, minced
¼ teaspoon ground coriander
1 teaspoon ground caraway
2–3 teaspoons water
Olive oil

In a food processor, process the pepper flakes with the garlic paste, coriander, caraway, 2 teaspoons water, and 1 to 2 tablespoons olive oil to make a thick paste (more water and olive oil may be needed). Pack tightly in a small jar and top with some olive oil to cover. Keep in the refrigerator.

Harissa keeps for 6 months or more.

Makes a generous ⅓ cup.

NOTE: If you are using dried New Mexican chili peppers, remove the stems and seeds and soak in warm water for 10 to 20 minutes. Wrap them in cheesecloth and press to remove as much water as possible, then proceed as described for crushed red pepper without adding any water.

Tunisian Carrot Salad

THIS IS MY VERSION of the carrot salad that you will find in most North African cuisines. It is very easy to make, delicious, and full of beta-carotene. Serve it as an appetizer or with grilled meat or fish.

1 pound carrots

2 garlic cloves, minced, or 1 teaspoon Roasted
   Garlic and Pepper Paste (page 88)

2–3 tablespoons sherry or red wine vinegar

½–1 teaspoon Harissa, or to taste (page 83)

1 teaspoon ground caraway

1 teaspoon Salted Fresh Coriander (page 95)

3–4 tablespoons virgin olive oil

Salt to taste

A few sprigs of parsley, 3–4 slices of Preserved
   Lemons (page 79), and a few black Kalamata
   olives, for garnish

OPPOSITE
Harissa

Wash, peel, and cut the carrots in half lengthwise. Chop coarsely and transfer to a saucepan. Cover the carrots with cold water and bring the water to a boil. Reduce the heat and simmer the carrots until tender, about 20 to 30 minutes. Drain, then mash with a fork in a large bowl. Mix in 2 tablespoons of the vinegar, ½ teaspoon of the *harissa,* the garlic, caraway, salted coriander, and olive oil. Stir well and taste. Season with a little salt or more vinegar and *harissa* if needed. Let cool completely and refrigerate for at least 3 hours or overnight before serving.

Decorate with the parsley, chopped preserved lemon, and olives just before serving.
Serves 4.

Hot Pepper and Onion Paste (*Hrous*)

THIS DELICIOUS HOT PEPPER PASTE, a specialty of southern Tunisia, is different from *harissa* in two significant ways: It is made with onions instead of garlic and it contains more spices. In the traditional recipe for this flavorful paste, large quantities of onions are sprinkled with salt and turmeric and left to ferment in clay jars for about three months before the chili peppers and spices are mixed in. The following much simpler version is based on Paula Wolfert's recipe, included in her marvelous book, *The Cooking of the Eastern Mediterranean*.

Use Hrous to flavor tomato sauces, stews, soups, and—of course—couscous dishes. Also mix a little Hrous with olive oil and use it for bread-dipping at the table.

½ pound onions, thickly sliced

3–4 tablespoons coarse salt

⅔ teaspoon turmeric

12–15 dried New Mexican chili peppers
(see Mail-Order Sources, page 134)

1½ teaspoons coriander seed

2 tablespoons caraway seed

½ teaspoon ground cinnamon

1 tablespoon dried rosebuds (see Mail-Order
Sources, page 134; optional)

4–5 tablespoons olive oil

In a deep dish, combine the onions with the salt and turmeric. Let stand for about 3 days, until the onions become very soft. Transfer the onions to a sieve lined with cheesecloth and let them drain. Gather the ends of the cloth and squeeze the onions to extract all of their liquid. You may find that this process works better if you divide the onions into batches.

Cut off the stems and discard the seeds of the chili peppers. Cut the peppers into flat pieces and toast over low heat in an ungreased frying pan, removing them from the pan as soon as they start to give off their aroma, about 10 minutes. Let cool a little. In a blender, spice grinder, or clean coffee grinder, in batches, grind the toasted chilies with the coriander, caraway, cinnamon, and rosebuds.

Combine the spice mixture, drained onions, and olive oil, and, wearing rubber gloves, knead to mix well. Pack into a 1½-cup jar and top with more olive oil.

Hrous will keep for about 3 to 5 months in the refrigerator.

Makes 1 cup.

Pickled long green chili peppers are served as *meze* (appetizers) with ouzo in Greek *tavernas,* and a jar of pickled peppers is part of most Greek pantries. But because I don't particularly like whole pickled chili peppers, I use them only chopped or in paste form.

Add a little Green Chili Pepper Paste to salad dressings, spreads—such as eggplant or roasted pepper—and marinades.

½ pound long green chili peppers	4 large garlic cloves, peeled and halved lengthwise
2 tablespoons coriander seed	2 cups distilled white vinegar
2 tablespoons white mustard seed	1 cup red wine vinegar

Wash and dry the peppers. Make 1 or 2 incisions in each pepper (depending on their size), so that the vinegar will penetrate them quickly. Pack them tightly in a 1-quart jar and sprinkle with the coriander and mustard. Add the garlic and pour in the vinegars, which should cover them completely.

Let stand for about 4 weeks, shaking occasionally. Take the peppers out of the liquid, cut off the stems, and discard most of the seeds. Place the peppers in a food processor with 2 tablespoons of the liquid and process to obtain a smooth paste. Place in a jar, cover tightly, and keep in a cool place or in the refrigerator.

Green Chili Pepper Paste will keep for a year or more.

Makes 1½ to 2 cups.

Roasted Garlic and Pepper Paste

WHOLE HEADS OF GARLIC roasted with meat or poultry are common in recipes from Italy and the South of France. The garlic—which turns into a fragrant paste when roasted—is spread over the hot meat, giving it a great taste. But because garlic needs at least an hour to cook, it is much more convenient to keep garlic paste on hand in the refrigerator than to prepare it from scratch each time you want to use it.

Use this paste in sauces, salads (see Tunisian Carrot Salad, page 85), and marinades for meat, fish, poultry, or game. You can also make garlic-pepper olive oil by adding 1 tablespoon of garlic paste per cup of extra-virgin olive oil. Let stand for two to three days, shaking occasionally before using.

10 whole heads of garlic
Approximately ½ cup olive oil
Sea salt

1½–2 teaspoons Near Eastern or Aleppo
    crushed red pepper (see Mail-Order Sources,
    page 134) or red pepper flakes

Preheat the oven to 350°F.

Cut about ¾ inch off the top of each garlic head and pour about a teaspoon of olive oil over the exposed flesh. Season with a little salt, then wrap 2 or 3 heads together in aluminum foil. Bake in the oven for 1 to 1½ hours or until very soft.

Let cool a little, then open the foil and squeeze the garlic cloves from their husks into a small bowl. Add the red pepper, stir well to mix, and transfer to a jar, pressing well so that no air pockets are formed. Top with olive oil and seal with the lid.

Roasted Garlic and Pepper Paste will keep for 2 to 3 months in the refrigerator.

Makes about 1½ cups.

Roasted Garlic Sauce

MADE WITH ROASTED GARLIC AND PEPPER PASTE, this is a mild variation of Greek *skordalia* and Middle Eastern *tarator,* both of which are traditionally prepared with stronger-tasting raw garlic. Even people who say they don't like garlic have liked this sauce.

Serve this sauce with crudités or as a sauce with sautéed, steamed, or grilled fish or vegetables. It is especially good with beets and steamed potatoes.

1 thick slice good-quality white bread, crusts removed, soaked in water and squeezed dry (about ½ cup)

½ cup freshly mashed potatoes

3–4 tablespoons Roasted Garlic and Pepper Paste (page 88)

⅔ cup mixed chopped walnuts and lightly toasted pine nuts

⅓–½ cup lemon juice

½ cup olive oil

Salt and freshly ground black pepper, to taste

Place the bread, potatoes, Roasted Garlic and Pepper Paste, and nuts in the bowl of a food processor. Pour in 3 tablespoons lemon juice and process until the mixture is smooth. Add the olive oil and taste. Adjust the seasoning with more lemon juice, salt, and freshly ground pepper.

Roasted Garlic Sauce will keep for up to 2 weeks in the refrigerator.

Makes about 2½ cups.

Romesco Tomato Sauce

BAKED TOMATOES, onions, peppers, and garlic are the base for the classic Spanish Romesco sauce in which all of the ingredients are baked in the oven instead of being cooked on top of the stove. After I saw the chef and owner of the elegant restaurant Flora in Barcelona prepare this incredibly rich sauce for the first time, I immediately changed the way I make tomato sauces.

Romesco Tomato Sauce is excellent in soups, on pizzas, and in pasta sauces. Use to give extra flavor to special dishes.

1 large onion, unpeeled and halved	2 green bell peppers
Olive oil, to coat the vegetables	1 fresh chili pepper, or more to taste
1 whole garlic head	5–6 large red beefsteak tomatoes (about 3 pounds)

Preheat the oven to 450°F. Rub the onion halves with olive oil, place in a pan, and bake for 20 minutes.

Meanwhile, cut off the top of the garlic and drizzle with a little olive oil. Wash and dry all of the other vegetables and coat them with olive oil. Place in the pan with the half-baked onion and bake for 45 minutes, or until the onion, garlic, peppers, and tomatoes are soft.

Press the garlic to extract the baked cloves. Pass all of the vegetables through a food mill fitted with the medium disk. Add the roasted garlic to the mill and pass it through with the rest.

Place the pulp in a deep 12-x-9-inch baking pan, lower the oven temperature to 300°F., and bake the sauce for about 2 hours, stirring twice, until it gets very thick.

Let the sauce cool, then pack in jars, pressing well to avoid air pockets. Top with a thin film of olive oil and store in the refrigerator.

Romesco Tomato Sauce will keep for 3 to 4 weeks.

Makes about 2 cups.

Tʜɪs ɪs ᴍʏ ᴏᴡɴ ᴠᴇʀꜱɪᴏɴ of the cracked olives in spicy Seville orange juice and olive oil that I tasted in a Lebanese restaurant in Athens. I have combined orange and lemon juice because Seville oranges, unfortunately, are not widely available.

14 ounces freshly cured green olives in brine,
  preferably Greek cracked olives

2 teaspoons Harissa (page 83)

4 tablespoons lemon juice (about 1½ lemons)

2 tablespoons orange juice (about ½ orange)

1 cup virgin olive oil

Zest from 1 orange

2 garlic cloves, quartered lengthwise

Wash the olives thoroughly under running water. Drain them well in a colander and on paper towels.

In a bowl, mix the *harissa* with the lemon and orange juices. Add the olive oil and whisk well. Pack the olives in layers in a 3-cup jar, placing orange zest and pieces of garlic between each layer of olives. Pour the olive oil mixture over them. If the olives are not completely covered, top with a little more olive oil. Seal and set aside at room temperature for 1 to 2 days. Store in the refrigerator. One hour before serving, take out as many as you need and let stand at room temperature.

Green Olives with Harissa and Orange will keep in the refrigerator for up to 2 months.

Makes 3 cups.

Sautéed Black Olives

Archestratus, the first known cookbook writer, lived in Sicily in the fourth century B.C. (when Sicily was a province of Greece). In his *Gastronomy,* he wrote: "Let them serve you with wrinkled, over-ripe olives." Like their forbears, modern Greeks adore black olives that are cured with coarse sea salt, lightly oiled, and sprinkled with savory, oregano, and rosemary. But these olives have to be consumed within seven to ten days, because they don't keep well (extra salt preserves the ones we find in stores).

In North Africa olives are dried in the sun and last all winter. In Pulia in southern Italy, the local small, black olives are sautéed without being cured and are then sprinkled with coarse salt and served warm as an appetizer. In this recipe, freshly cured olives are sautéed with onions, as is the custom in the Peloponnese, in southern mainland Greece.

Serve these Sautéed Black Olives as an appetizer or snack or chop and add to salads, tomato sauces, and vegetable and meat stews.

1¼ pounds freshly cured or fleshy wrinkled
  black Greek olives (often called Thassos olives)
Olive oil, for sautéing

1 medium onion, sliced
1 tablespoon dried savory or a mixture of
  dried oregano and thyme

Soak the olives in warm water overnight. Change the water in the morning and taste the olives. If they are still very salty, leave for another 2 to 3 hours (see Note). Drain and let dry completely on paper towels.

Heat about ½ inch olive oil in a frying pan. Add the onion and sauté for 30 seconds. Add the olives and sauté for 8 to 10 minutes until soft and shiny. Transfer the olives and onion to a colander with a slotted spoon. Add the herbs, toss well, and let cool completely. Transfer the mixture to a 1-quart jar, cover, and refrigerate.

Sautéed Black Olives will keep for 3 to 4 weeks. Let them stand at room temperature for 2 to 3 hours before serving.

Makes 1¼ pounds.

NOTE: If you can find ripe, freshly harvested black olives, place them in a basket set over a bucket or in a large bowl. Sprinkle generously with coarse salt and let them stand for 6 to 8 days, tossing twice a day. When their flesh turns black all the way through to the kernel, rinse them briefly with running water, drain, and let them dry on paper towels overnight. Then sauté as described above.

Uncured or freshly cured olives can also be frozen. They should be defrosted before sautéing.

Herbs Preserved in Salt

Some years ago, a friend gave me a recipe for a mixture of chopped herbs and salt that could be kept, almost indefinitely, in the refrigerator. The original recipe called for ½ pound each of parsley, celery, carrot, and leek. I omitted the carrot, since it contributed little in terms of flavor, and doubled the amount of leek. The resulting paste, mixed with salt, lends flavor and aroma to sauces and soups. As the mixture is very salty, it is unlikely that you will need to add more salt to any dish in which you use it.

You will need kitchen scales to measure the ingredients for this recipe. If not calculated exactly, the mixture will spoil.

Add about 1 tablespoon Preserved Herbs in Salt to every 4 cups of soup (such as chicken, vegetable, or legume), as well as to sauces you make with meat or poultry demi-glace.

3 ounces flat-leaf parsley leaves, most stems cut off, washed and dried	6 ounces leeks, white part only, sliced
3 ounces celery leaves, most stems cut off, washed and dried	2½ ounces sea salt

Place the herbs and the leeks in the bowl of a food processor and process—starting and stopping the motor—to obtain a paste. Empty the herb mixture into a nonreactive bowl, add the salt, and mix very well. Pack in a 1-pint glass jar.

Herbs Preserved in Salt will keep for up to 1 year in the refrigerator.

Makes 2 cups.

VARIATION: Substitute dill or fennel tops for the celery.

Fresh coriander (also known as cilantro) is essential to many Middle Eastern and North African dishes. Because it is sometimes difficult to find—and very difficult to store—it is a good idea to keep a jar of salted chopped leaves on hand. The flavor is slightly different but still very good.

Salted Fresh Coriander will add an extra punch to any fresh or steamed vegetable salad, as well as to chicken soup. It is an essential ingredient for Tunisian Carrot Salad (see page 85).

6 ounces fresh coriander leaves, most stems cut off, washed and dried
$1\frac{1}{4}$ ounces sea salt

Place the coriander leaves in the bowl of a food processor and process—starting and stopping the motor—to obtain a paste. Empty the mixture into a nonreactive bowl, add the salt, and mix thoroughly. Pack into a 1-cup glass jar.

Salted Fresh Coriander will keep for 4 to 5 weeks in the refrigerator before it starts to lose its flavor.

Makes 1 cup.

Green Tomato and Mint Relish

Unripe fruits, such as grapes and plums, are often cooked with spring lamb throughout the Mediterranean. Their particular tartness complements the rich flavor of the lamb beautifully. This combination must be very old, from a time before lemons were available.

My Green Tomato and Mint Relish is inspired by these old combinations. Serve it with cold smoked meats or grilled lamb, poultry, or game. It is also very good served with blue cheeses, such as Roquefort, Gorgonzola, and Stilton.

2 pounds green tomatoes (or unripe seedless grapes or unripe green plums)

½ cup white wine vinegar (only if you are using tomatoes)

½ cup water (or 1 cup for grapes and plums)

3 sprigs fresh mint

1 cup cider vinegar

1–1½ cups sugar

1 small fresh green chili pepper, cut in half lengthwise

2 teaspoons dried mint

Wash, dry, and peel the green tomatoes. Cut in half, remove and discard the hard stem, and dice the flesh, removing most of the seeds. (If you are using unripe grapes or plums you need only to wash and dry them.)

Place the green tomatoes (or grapes or plums) in a nonreactive pan with the white wine vinegar, water, and fresh mint. Cook for about 15 minutes over high heat, stirring from time to time, then let cool a little. (At this stage the plums will have softened and you will be able to remove their pits.) Add the cider vinegar, 1 cup sugar for the tomatoes (1½ cups for the other fruits), and the chili pepper. Turn the heat to medium and cook for 1 hour, stirring occasionally.

Reduce the heat, add 1 teaspoon dried mint, and simmer for another 20 minutes, until very soft. Remove from the heat, add the remaining teaspoon of dried mint, stir, and transfer the dish to sterilized jars, leaving ¼ inch for space at the top of the jars. Cover while still hot and let cool before transferring to the refrigerator. If you want to store the jars of relish in a cupboard, process for 10 minutes in a water bath (see page 15).

Green Tomato and Mint Relish will keep for 2 to 3 months in the refrigerator or for 1 year if sealed in a water bath.

Makes about 1½ cups.

Spring is artichoke season around the Mediterranean, but artichokes are so popular that we try to preserve them to eat throughout the year. Small artichokes are commonly preserved in brine, but I have my own way of preserving fried artichokes in olive oil, then serving them as an appetizer or in artichoke omelets.

Don't be frightened by the amount of virgin olive oil called for in this recipe. It is not wasted because you can use it in salad dressings when you have finished eating the artichokes. Or you can heat it with additional chopped garlic and some chopped chili pepper and capers, then toss with freshly cooked pasta, sprinkle with chopped parsley or dill, and serve. The garlic and capers give this oil a delicious flavor.

2 large lemons

7 medium artichokes (2½ inches in diameter; see Note)

Olive oil, for frying

Flour, for dredging

Sea salt to taste

3–4 garlic cloves, unpeeled

2 tablespoons capers, rinsed in cold water and drained well on paper towels

1 dried mild chili pepper, cut in half lengthwise

1½–2 cups virgin olive oil

Prepare the artichokes. Pour about 1 quart water into a bowl and add the juice of 1 lemon. Cut off the hard outer leaves of one artichoke, then keep snapping off leaves until you are left with a soft cone formed by the light green inner leaves and the heart.

Cut the second lemon in half and rub the cut surfaces of the artichoke to prevent discoloration. Trim the green top of the cone and remove the choke with a teaspoon. Halve the artichoke lengthwise and, after rubbing the cut surface with lemon, place it in a bowl of lemon water. Repeat with the remaining artichokes.

Heat about ½ inch of olive oil in a frying pan. Dredge artichokes in flour. Shake well to get rid of the excess flour, then fry the pieces in the oil until soft, about 3 minutes, turning once. Place on paper towels to drain, then salt lightly. Discard the frying oil, wipe the frying pan with paper towels, and add 2 tablespoons fresh olive oil. Crush the garlic cloves and sauté for 30 seconds in the oil. Remove from the heat.

Pack the artichokes, garlic and its oil, capers, and chili pepper in a 3-cup glass jar. Cover completely with virgin olive oil. Let cool, then refrigerate.

Fried Artichokes with Garlic in Olive Oil will keep for 4 to 5 weeks. Let stand for 1 to 2 hours at room temperature, then sprinkle with lemon juice before serving.

Makes 3 cups.

NOTE: If you can find only large artichokes, you can quarter them.

Yogurt Cheese in Olive Oil with Chili Pepper and Herbs

Armenians, lebanese, and other inhabitants of the Middle East like to prepare a simple fresh cheese by draining some of the liquid from yogurt. In the past, if this cheese was not going to be eaten the day it was made, it was formed into small balls, heavily salted, and dried in the sun. As there was no refrigeration, the cheese had to be dried completely so it could be stored in clay jars. To be eaten, the little balls were pounded in a mortar and sprinkled on salads and vegetable dishes.

In my modern recipe the light and faintly tart yogurt cheese is dried slightly in the refrigerator, preserved in olive oil scented with a chili pepper and herbs, then refrigerated again until ready to use. This treatment is also delicious if you use small pieces of Pecorino, Manchego, or any soft goat cheese. It is excellent with Cretan Barley Paximadia (page 58) topped with tomato and onions.

2 pounds thick sheep's milk yogurt
  (see Mail-Order Sources, page 134)
3 teaspoons coarsely ground black pepper
3–4 teaspoons sea salt
2 teaspoons dried oregano

1 teaspoon dried savory or thyme
1 small dried chili pepper, cut in half lengthwise
1 bay leaf
1½–2 cups olive oil

Combine the yogurt, pepper, and salt in a bowl. Lay a double layer of cheesecloth or a kitchen towel in a bowl, pour the yogurt in it, tie the ends together, and suspend over a bowl to drain in a cool place. Leave for 12 hours.

Open the cheesecloth and, 1 tablespoon at a time, press and roll the soft cheese between your palms to form little spheres. Place the spheres on a plate and refrigerate, uncovered, overnight to dry out a little.

Pack the cheese in a 3-cup jar, sprinkle with the herbs, and place the chili pepper and bay leaf in the jar. Pour enough olive oil over the cheese to cover it. Seal and store in the refrigerator.

Yogurt Cheese will keep for 2 to 3 months.

Makes about 32 little balls.

Grilled Bell Peppers in Garlic Olive Oil

Although bell peppers are New World vegetables and became part of the Mediterranean food basket only at the end of the 16th century, it is hard to imagine how we did without them. Today they are added to sauces, fried, and stuffed with rice, vegetables, meat, or fish. They are also grilled and eaten simply with bread and cheese, or as an accompaniment to meat, poultry, or fish. Grilled Peppers Stuffed with Hot Pepper and Feta Spread (see following page) makes a very interesting appetizer.

3 red bell peppers	¾ cup virgin olive oil
3 green bell peppers	1 tablespoon Roasted Garlic and Pepper Paste (page 88)
2 yellow bell peppers	½ teaspoon freshly ground black pepper

Wash and dry the peppers. Cut them lengthwise into thirds, then seed them and discard the stems. Each pepper should yield 3 quite flat pieces.

Position an oven rack about 5 inches from the heat source, line the rack with aluminum foil, and lay the pepper pieces, skin side up, on the foil. Broil the peppers for about 20 minutes, until their skins are black and blistered.

Place the peppers in a bowl and cover with plastic wrap. Leave for about 15 minutes, then peel off the blackened skin.

In a bowl, whisk the oil with the Roasted Garlic and Pepper Paste. Place alternating layers of green, red, and yellow pepper pieces in a 3-cup jar, pouring a little sauce between each layer. Make sure to press down on the peppers so that no air pockets form. Top with the remaining sauce, adding a little more olive oil if needed to cover the peppers completely. Seal and store in the refrigerator.

Grilled Bell Peppers in Garlic Olive Oil will keep for 2 to 3 weeks in the refrigerator.

Makes 3 cups.

Grilled Peppers Stuffed with Hot Pepper and Feta Spread

Here is an easy last-minute appetizer made from two items in your Mediterranean pantry. The combination of roasted bell peppers and pepper-flavored feta cheese is delicious.

    5 pieces Grilled Bell Peppers in Garlic Olive Oil (previous page)
    1 cup Hot Pepper and Feta Spread (page 104)
    Sprigs of fresh coriander, for garnish (optional)

Drain the grilled pepper pieces thoroughly and cut each in half lengthwise. Place a teaspoon of Hot Pepper and Feta Spread at the end of a pepper strip and roll it up lengthwise. Secure with a toothpick. Refrigerate for 1 to 2 hours before serving. Decorate with fresh coriander and serve.

Makes about 30 rolls.

Grilled Vegetables in Olive Oil

Sicilians have taught us the value of simple preparations to bring out the fresh flavors of vegetables. And there is nothing simpler and more delicious than sliced eggplant, zucchini, and peppers grilled over a charcoal fire, sprinkled with chopped garlic and parsley, and drizzled with fruity olive oil. In fact, women in tourist-frequented Sicilian villages often sell their grilled vegetables in olive oil to visitors.

To serve Grilled Vegetables in Olive Oil, drain the vegetable slices and sprinkle with chopped parsley and garlic. Or dice the vegetables, mix with minced garlic and parsley, toss with freshly cooked pasta, and serve warm or at room temperature.

2 large eggplants (about 1½ pounds)

Sea salt

4 zucchini (about 1 pound)

1 large onion

1½ cups virgin olive oil, plus extra to
   baste the vegetables

2 garlic cloves, chopped

Freshly ground black pepper

1 tablespoon Roasted Garlic and Pepper Paste
   (page 88)

3 green or red bell peppers, grilled and peeled
   as described on page 100

Wash, dry, and cut the eggplants lengthwise into ¼-inch slices. Sprinkle each slice with salt on both sides, then leave in a colander for about 30 minutes. Wash the eggplant slices under cold water and pat dry with paper towels.

Cut the zucchini lengthwise into ¼-inch slices. Cut the onion crosswise into ¼-inch-thick slices. Baste all the vegetable slices on both sides with olive oil. Sprinkle with the chopped garlic and freshly ground black pepper and leave to marinate for about 2 hours.

Position a charcoal grill or broiler rack 5 inches from the heat source and preheat. Grill or broil the eggplant, zucchini, and onion for about 15–20 minutes, turning once, until soft.

Arrange alternate vegetable slices, starting with eggplant, in a short-sided, wide-mouthed 5- to 6-cup glass jar. Whisk 1 tablespoon of Garlic and Pepper paste into 1 cup olive oil and drizzle over the vegetables. Continue with slices of onion, zucchini, pepper, and so forth, sprinkling each layer lightly with salt and pepper and drizzling with the garlic-flavored olive oil. When all of the vegetables are packed, press well to get rid of any air pockets and top with the rest of the olive oil, making sure to cover the vegetables completely. Seal and store in the refrigerator.

Grilled Vegetables in Olive Oil will keep for a month.

Makes about 3 cups.

I AM NOT PARTICULARLY fond of cold pasta, especially when it is served directly from the refrigerator, as is the case at most salad bars and take-out restaurants. It is very convenient, however, to be able to cook pasta, drain it, then simply mix it with a cold sauce that you have made previously, such as the one that follows.

This sauce is at its best when tossed with warm pasta, sprinkled with freshly chopped parsley, basil, or dill, and, if desired, Parmesan cheese, then eaten right away. It is also good at room temperature.

1 cup virgin olive oil	1 cup Kalamata olives, pitted and coarsely chopped
2 cups thinly sliced fresh mushrooms	1 cup green olives (preferably Greek cracked olives),
1 small fresh chili pepper, chopped	pitted and coarsely chopped
3 garlic cloves, chopped	½ cup salted capers (see Mail-Order Sources, page
⅓ cup plus 1 tablespoon sherry vinegar	134), soaked in warm water and rinsed well
2 tablespoons dry white wine	5 sun-dried tomatoes, chopped
1 teaspoon dried Mediterranean oregano	Salt and freshly ground black pepper to taste

In a frying pan, warm 2 tablespoons of the olive oil. Add the mushrooms and sauté over high heat until soft. Add the chili pepper and garlic and sauté briefly, being careful not to let the garlic take on any color.

Remove the mushroom mixture from the heat, let cool a little, then add the vinegar and wine. Sprinkle with the oregano, transfer to a 1-quart jar, cover, and let stand for a day. Mix in the chopped olives, capers, sun-dried tomatoes, and the remaining olive oil. Cover again, shake well, and taste. The sauce should have a robust flavor. Adjust the seasoning by adding a little salt and pepper.

Store in a cool, dark place or in the refrigerator. Let stand at room temperature for 1 hour and shake well before serving.

This sauce will keep for about 2 to 3 weeks in the refrigerator.

Makes about 3½ cups sauce, enough for 2 pounds pasta.

Hot Pepper and Feta Spread

Hot pepper and feta spread is served as an appetizer in Salonica, the second largest Greek city, with crudités or with Cretan Barley Paximadia (see page 58) or Olive Oil, Pepper, and Ouzo Biscuits (see page 63). You can also use it to stuff grilled peppers (see page 101), and as a topping for baked potatoes.

1 red bell pepper
3 tablespoons olive oil, plus extra to
  top the jar

½–1 teaspoon Near Eastern or Aleppo crushed red
  pepper (see Mail-Order Sources, page 134) or
  red pepper flakes
2½ cups (about 1 pound) crumbed feta cheese

Wash, dry, and seed the pepper, then cut into ½-inch rings. In a frying pan, warm the oil, then add the pepper rings and red pepper and sauté until the pepper rings are soft, about 6 to 10 minutes.

Place the crumbed feta and the sautéed peppers with their oil in the bowl of a food processor. Process, pulsing the motor on and off, until the mixture becomes a smooth spread. Transfer the spread to jars, pressing down on it to eliminate all air pockets. Top with a thin film of olive oil and store in the refrigerator.

Hot Pepper and Feta Spread will keep for 3 to 4 weeks.

Makes about 3 cups.

Berber Lamb in Olive Oil

In the berber villages of southern Tunisia, on the edge of the Sahara Desert, people live very frugally. During the growing season they try to preserve as much food as they can—usually by salting and drying in the blazing sun—to sustain them during the dry months when there is hardly anything for their sheep and goats to graze on. For example, they often preserve little pieces of meat or fish to cook in their highly spiced vegetable stews and to add flavor to the couscous, their staple food, with which the stew is served.

The following is my own adaptation of a recipe for preserved lamb given to me by Aziza Ben Tanfous, the curator of the Houmt Souk National Museum in Djerba and an expert on Berber food.

In Mani, the southernmost peninsula of the Peloponnese, in Greece, people prepare pork in a similar way, but with just coarse salt. The half-dried pork pieces are then kept in olive oil until they are used.

Add pieces of Berber Lamb to vegetable stews, tagines, sauces, and soups to give them extra flavor.

1²/₃ pounds boned lamb leg and saddle	²/₃ teaspoon turmeric
3 tablespoons coarse sea salt	2 tablespoons Harissa (page 83)
2 teaspoons dried mint	2 garlic cloves, minced
2 teaspoons caraway seed	Approximately 1½ cups olive oil

Wash and dry the lamb. Cut into ¼-inch-thick slices, then press with the palm of your hand to flatten.

In a spice grinder or clean coffee grinder, or in a mortar, grind the salt, mint, caraway seed, and turmeric to obtain a fine powder. Transfer to a bowl and add the *harissa* and garlic. Add 2 to 3 teaspoons or more olive oil to make a thick paste.

Rub the lamb slices with the paste on all sides. Transfer to a pan, cover with plastic wrap, and let sit for 2 to 3 hours at room temperature or overnight in the refrigerator. (If you have refrigerated the lamb, leave it at room temperature for about 1 hour before proceeding further.)

Preheat the oven to 200°F. Place the lamb slices on the oven rack and let them dry for 2 hours. Turn the lamb and leave in the oven for another 1½ to 2 hours, until it is firm and cooked through.

In a small, deep frying pan, warm about 2 inches of oil. Add the lamb and deep-fry for 3 to 5 minutes, depending on the size of the pieces. Remove and drain on paper towels to cool slightly.

Pass the frying oil through a fine-meshed sieve lined with a double layer of cheesecloth.

Pack the lamb slices in a 1-quart jar. Pour 1 cup of the frying oil over them and top with about another cup of fresh olive oil. Seal and keep in the refrigerator.

Berber Lamb in Olive Oil will keep for up to 6 months.

Makes 1 quart.

Pickled Huevos Haminados

Sᴇᴘʜᴀʀᴅɪᴄ ᴊᴇᴡs who lived near the Mediterranean used to prepare *huevos haminados* (baked eggs) on Fridays to serve on the Sabbath. Originally these eggs were placed in a pot filled with onion skins and water, then baked in a communal oven. Later, the eggs were simmered for hours on top of the stove. The onion skins darken the whites of the eggs and give them a very distinctive flavor. When pickled, *huevos haminados* are simply delicious.

Serve Pickled Huevos Haminados as an appetizer or slice or chop and add to any salad of raw or cooked vegetables.

6 large, very fresh eggs

Skins of 10 medium purple onions, or

   5 large purple onions, quartered

2 medium purple onions, quartered, and

   1 large purple onion, sliced

2 tablespoons olive oil

1¼ cups white wine vinegar

2 tablespoons sugar

3 large sprigs wild fennel or 1–2 fennel bulbs, sliced

2 tablespoons coriander seed

1 fresh or dried red chili pepper, halved

   lengthwise

Place the eggs in a large pot with the onion skins, whole onions, and quartered onions. Cover with water, bring to a boil, then turn down the heat so the water just simmers. Pour in the olive oil, cover the pot, and cook for 4 hours, checking every now and then and adding a little water as the liquid in the pot evaporates.

Drain the eggs and cool under running water. Peel the eggs and place in a 1½-pint glass jar. Warm the vinegar with the sugar, stirring until the sugar dissolves. Place the fennel, coriander seed, onion slices, and chili pepper in the jar with the eggs. Top with the vinegar mixture, which should cover the eggs. Add extra vinegar if necessary. Let stand at room temperature for at least 3 weeks, shaking occasionally, before serving.

Pickled Huevos Haminados will keep for 6 months to 1 year in a cool place.

Makes 6.

IN THE SPRING, fresh green garlic, which looks very much like thick scallions, appears in farmer's markets all around the Mediterranean. It is delicious chopped and added to legume purées and salads in season and pickled to serve as an appetizer year-round. I make Pickled Green Garlic in a long, tall jar because it holds the long garlic shoots perfectly.

Serve Pickled Green Garlic as an appetizer or add it whole or chopped to fresh or cooked salads. It is excellent with steamed potatoes.

2 pounds fresh green garlic

1½ cups distilled white vinegar

2 tablespoons honey

1 teaspoon white mustard seed

2 tablespoons coriander seed

1½ tablespoons fennel seed

½ cup sherry vinegar

1 cup good-quality white wine vinegar

1 fresh or dried chili pepper, bruised

OVERLEAF
Preserved Grapevine Shoots with Raisins, Pickled Huevos Haminados, Sliced Turnip Pickles, Pickled Green Garlic, Pickled Octopus, and Pickled Cucumbers with Fennel and Green Olives

Cut and discard the tops of the green stems of the garlic so that it fits in a tall jar. Wash the garlic well, then dry and place in the jar.

In a medium saucepan, warm the distilled white vinegar with the honey, stirring with a wooden spoon until the honey dissolves. Let cool, then add the mustard, coriander, fennel, and sherry and white wine vinegars. Place the bruised chili pepper in the jar and top with the vinegar mixture, which should cover the garlic. Let stand at room temperature for 3 to 4 weeks before serving.

Pickled Green Garlic will keep for up to a year.

Makes 1 quart.

NOTE: This recipe can also be used to pickle baby leeks that are no thicker than your little finger, ramps (wild leeks, sometimes available at farmer's markets in the spring), or scallions with bulbs.

Sliced Turnip Pickles

Turnips are cooked with carrots, lamb, and chicken in all kinds of North African couscous dishes. In Tunisia, turnips are also served fresh, very thinly sliced and marinated for a couple of hours in Seville orange juice (or a combination of lemon and orange juice).

These simple turnip pickles from Tunisia are as lovely to look at as they are delicious to eat. Beets are used here—as in many other Mediterranean preserves—for color, to turn the white turnip slices pink.

Serve as you would pickled cucumbers, as an accompaniment to cold meat and cheese sandwiches.

2 pounds turnips

4–5 cups white wine vinegar

2–4 tablespoons sugar

2 small uncooked beets, washed well, dried, and diced

2 fresh mild chili peppers

2 bay leaves

2 tablespoons coriander seed

Wash, dry, and peel the turnips. Slice them into ¼-inch-thick slices. In a nonreactive saucepan, warm 2 cups vinegar with the sugar until the sugar dissolves, using more or less sugar according to how acidic you like your pickles. Pack the turnip slices into a 1-quart jar and a ¾-quart jar. Divide the diced beets, chili peppers, bay leaves, coriander seed, and the warm vinegar-sugar mixture between the jars. Top with more vinegar to cover the turnip slices if necessary. Cover and keep in a cool place. Shake from time to time for the first 3 days. The pickles will be ready to eat after 4 to 5 days.

Sliced Turnip Pickles will keep well for 3 months or more in a cool, dark place.

Makes 1¾ quarts.

Octopus is prepared in several different ways and is eaten frequently in all Mediterranean countries. It is stewed, grilled, and pickled, and is often salted and left in the sun until completely dry. Dried octopuses are sold in the souks of Tunisia, along with small dried fish, like smelts. Both these dried sea creatures are soaked in water and added to the fish couscous dishes, and even to some meat couscous dishes—which brings to mind the ancient Greek and Roman fish sauce known as *garum,* or *liquamen* (see page 22).

Pickled octopus is one of the most common Greek appetizers; it is served with ouzo in *tavernas* all over the country.

To serve at home, drain and dress with olive oil and sprinkle with dried savory or oregano.

1 medium octopus (about 2 pounds), cleaned

4 bay leaves

1 tablespoon dried savory

1 tablespoon coriander seed

1 small fresh or dried chili pepper

3–3½ cups good-quality red wine vinegar

Olive oil, to top the jar

Add 2 quarts water and 1 bay leaf to a large pot and bring the water to a boil. Add the octopus and blanch briefly, until it becomes stiff and its color lightens, about 3 to 5 minutes.

Drain and cut off the legs with a sharp knife. Place the cut-up octopus in a 1½-quart jar with the remaining bay leaves, savory, coriander seed, and chili pepper.

Cover the octopus completely with the vinegar. Add 1 inch of olive oil. Cover and keep at room temperature. It will be ready to serve after 1 week.

Pickled Octopus keeps for 2 to 3 weeks at room temperature, and 2 to 3 months in the refrigerator.

Makes 1½ quarts.

Pickled Cucumbers with Fennel and Green Olives

WANDERING AROUND in the endless alleys of the covered bazaar in Istanbul one afternoon, I saw a young man carrying a tin bucket full of large pickled cucumbers. He would stop at each stand, selling one to each shopkeeper, who would eat it immediately, just as many of us would snack on candy or chocolate.

Pickles play a very important role on the Mediterranean table, as they are part of most *meze* assortments, the little dishes served at midday or in the evening, usually with a milky glass of ouzo, raki, or pernod—mixed with ice water.

The recipe that follows is my own version of Algerian pickles I once ate in Paris. Serve with cold meat and poultry, as an appetizer, and in Istanbul Salad (see following page).

1 pound small to medium cucumbers, washed and drained (see Note)

3 sweet frying peppers, stemmed, seeded, and halved lengthwise

2 large carrots, quartered lengthwise

2 small fennel bulbs, cut into thick slices

Approximately 1 cup coarse sea salt

2½–3 cups white wine vinegar

2 tablespoons sugar

10–12 green olives in brine, preferably Greek cracked olives, soaked in water for 15 minutes, rinsed well, and drained

4 large sprigs wild fennel or dill

1 fresh or dried chili pepper

2 tablespoons white mustard seed

2 tablespoons coriander seed

Place the cucumbers, frying peppers, carrots, and fennel in layers in a colander, sprinkling each layer generously with salt. Cover with aluminum foil and let stand overnight. The next day rinse well under cold running water, drain, and dry on paper towels.

In a nonreactive saucepan, warm 1 cup vinegar with the sugar, stirring until the sugar has dissolved. Let cool.

Pack the vegetables in a 1½-quart jar, then add the olives, sprigs of fennel, chili pepper, and mustard and coriander seed. Pour the vinegar-sugar mixture and enough of the remaining vinegar into the jar to cover the vegetables. Leave at room temperature for 3 to 4 weeks before serving.

Pickled Cucumbers will keep for up to a year in a cool, dark place. Make sure that the pickles are always completely covered with vinegar.

Makes 1½ quarts.

NOTE: Instead of using regular pickling cucumbers, I prefer to pickle long, thin, unripe cucumbers that I order from the growers from Crete who sell their cucumbers at my neighborhood farmer's market.

Istanbul Salad

SOME *tavernas* in Athens call this mixed winter salad Istanbul Salad. I don't know if it actually originated in Istanbul, or if it is the invention of one of the many Greek cooks who in the 1950s came back to Greece from Istanbul, a city Greeks still call Constantinople.

1 cup mixed chopped Pickled Cucumbers
  with Fennel and Green Olives (previous page)
2–3 cups finely shredded cabbage, washed
  in cold water and drained well
½ cup chopped celery
1 large carrot, shredded
2 tablespoons chopped dill

3 tablespoons chopped flat-leaf parsley
½–1 teaspoon minced fresh chili pepper
2–3 tablespoons vinegar brine from
  the Pickled Cucumbers
4–5 tablespoons extra-virgin olive oil
Sea salt, to taste

In a large serving bowl, combine the chopped pickles, cabbage, celery, carrot, dill, parsley, and chili pepper. Make the dressing by whisking together the vinegar brine and olive oil, then pour the dressing over the salad. Season with salt, toss well, and cover with plastic wrap. Refrigerate for 1 to 2 hours before serving.

Serves 4.

Preserved Grapevine Shoots with Raisins

In APRIL, when the new grapevine shoots start sprouting their long spiral stems and their first leaves, Greeks like to cut a few, blanch them in boiling salted water, and serve them as a salad with fruity olive oil and fresh lemon juice. In the weekly Athenian neighborhood farmer's markets, one can occasionally find these grapevine shoots—at exorbitant prices. But people love them so much that they disappear fast. As these tender shoots are strictly seasonal, Greeks like to pickle them so that they can enjoy them all year long.

Serve Grapevine Shoots with Raisins as an appetizer, or add to potato or mixed green salads. Also serve with cheeses that aren't too salty, such as Gruyère, and with cold meat, poultry, or fish.

1 pound tender grapevine shoots
Coarse sea salt
1½ cups distilled white vinegar
Approximately 1 cup good-quality
   white wine vinegar
4 tablespoons honey

1 tablespoon coriander seed
1 teaspoon fennel seed
1–2 dried chili peppers
½ cup black raisins
3 garlic cloves, halved lengthwise

Wash and dry the grapevine shoots. Bring a large pot of water to a boil, add a handful of salt and the shoots, and blanch for about 3 minutes. Drain thoroughly.

In a nonreactive saucepan, warm the distilled wine and vinegars with the honey, stirring with a wooden spoon until the honey dissolves. Remove the saucepan from the heat and add the coriander and fennel seed, chili peppers, and raisins. Let cool. Remove the spices and raisins from the vinegar with a slotted spoon and reserve.

Pack 1 layer of grapevine shoots in a 6-cup jar and sprinkle it with some of the reserved raisins and fennel and coriander seed. Continue until you have used all the shoots and spices. Add the chili peppers, then pour the vinegar into the jar to cover the shoots by ½ inch, adding a little more white wine vinegar if needed. Cover, place in a cool, dry place, and let macerate for 3 to 4 weeks before serving.

Preserved Grapevine Shoots with Raisins will keep for up to a year at room temperature. Makes 5 cups.

Dried Apricots in Samos Vin de Liqueur

In THE BOOK *La Gastronomie au Moyen Age* (*Gastronomy in the Middle Ages*) by O. Redon, F. Sabban, and S. Serventi, 150 French and Italian recipes from the 14th century are revised and translated for the modern cook. While flipping through it I noticed a dessert in which pears were macerated in the strong, sweet *vin de liqueur* of Samos. As this wine has a strong apricot and peach aroma, I decided to pair it with dried apricots instead of pears.

Don't be fooled by the very attractive, plump, yellow dried apricots you will find in the markets. They must be full of chemicals to be able to last long in that condition. Your best choice for flavor are the more leathery, dark, unsulphered, organically grown ones.

Serve one or two apricots in a small bowl or stemmed glass with a little of their juice, and more of the wine of Samos from the bottle. Or, for a more elegant dessert, chop and arrange the macerated apricots in a layer on top of a prebaked meringue disk and top with whipped cream and toasted almonds.

3 cups dried apricots
1½–2 cups Samos Vin de Liqueur, Pineau des Charentes, or Vernaccia from Sardinia

Wash and drain the apricots, then pack in a 1-pint jar. Pour the wine over them and let stand for at least 2 weeks before serving.

Dried Apricots in Samos Vin de Liqueur will keep for about a year in a cool place.
Makes 1 pint.

YOU WILL FIND more than one recipe that calls for dried figs in this book, but this is the only one requiring fresh figs—although the ones used here are small, hard, unripe figs that are not edible unless they are cooked. You will never savor the full sweetness of fresh figs unless you cut them from a tree somewhere near the shores of the Mediterranean in August. The people who live near the Mediterranean cook only unripe or dried figs, because they don't dare tamper with the perfect taste of fresh, late-summer figs.

2½ pounds unripe green figs
About ½ pound blanched whole almonds
1½ pounds sugar
1⅓ cups water
2 leaves rose geranium

1 teaspoon whole cloves
Juice of 1 lemon
1 teaspoon mastic (see Mail-Order Sources, page 134)

Wash and dry the figs. Insert an almond in the small hole in the rounded end at the bottom of each fig.

Place the sugar and 1⅓ cups water in a heavy-bottomed saucepan and bring to a boil. Add the geranium leaves, cloves, and figs. Simmer over very low heat until the figs are tender, about 30 minutes or more. Remove the figs with a slotted spoon, add the lemon juice to the syrup, and bring to a boil. Continue boiling the syrup until it thickens (reaches 220°F. on a candy thermometer). Add the mastic, stir well, and remove from the heat. Return the figs to the syrup, then transfer to sterilized jars, allow to cool, cover, and store in a cool place, or refrigerate, or seal in a water bath for 10 minutes and keep in a cool place (see page 15).

Green Fig Preserves will keep for 6 months to a year.

Makes 1½ quarts.

Rose Petal Jam

THIS JAM, common throughout the Middle East, is the specialty of many nuns in Greek convents, who prepare it using roses grown in their own gardens.

Rose Petal Jam can sound better than it looks, especially if you don't make it with the right kind of rose: the pink, semi-wild ones with an intense aroma. All other roses make tasteless jam. As they cook, most rose petals turn yellowish, and unless you use some food coloring or a little uncooked beet, the jam looks rather unattractive.

As the appropriate roses are hard to find, I have added some very fragrant dried rosebuds to the best aromatic rose petals available, and the results have been excellent. Some people add rose water to the finished jam, but I find that good-quality dried rosebuds give a more natural fragrance.

Serve Rose Petal Jam as a sauce for vanilla ice cream or thick yogurt, or spread on buttered toast.

6–7 cups rose petals, the most fragrant ones you can find, preferably *Rosa rugosa*

2 cups water

2½ cups sugar

3 tablespoons lemon juice

½ cup dried rosebuds, tied in a piece of cheesecloth (see Mail-Order Sources, page 134)

½ peeled, diced raw beet (tied in a piece of cheesecloth) or a few drops of red food coloring (optional)

Pick the petals from the flowers and snip off the whitish, hard ends. Wash the petals, then simmer them in 2 cups water over low heat until tender, about 6 to 8 minutes. Add the sugar and continue cooking, stirring often with a wooden spoon, for another 5 minutes. Add the lemon juice and dried rosebuds and cook for another 5 minutes or more, until the syrup thickens.

Remove from the heat and add the beet or food coloring. (If using the beet, stir a few times until it gives the desired color, then discard.) Let cool, then remove the dried rosebuds, squeeze to extract all juices, and discard.

Fill small sterilized jars with the jam and keep in the refrigerator or seal in a water bath for 10 minutes and keep in a cool place (see page 15).

Rose Petal Jam will keep for up to 6 months in the refrigerator or 1 year in a cool, dark place.

Makes 2 to 2½ cups.

Fond as all eastern Mediterraneans are of spoon sweets, we very seldom make any kind of preserve using the flesh of the orange. This is because orange flesh is very juicy and either dissolves—if cooked for a long time—or makes the syrup in which it is served spoil—if cooked briefly. Most orange or bitter orange preserves are, therefore, made using just the thick pith (white part of the skin).

In order to create this recipe, I had to develop an entire new technique that involves partly drying the orange slices. As an added prize, in the process of trying different drying times, I discovered that completely dried orange slices are very tasty as a snack (see Variation).

Use these orange slices to top tarts and pastry creams.

5 untreated oranges (about 1½ pounds total)	1 cinnamon stick, 1 inch long
3 cups sugar	1 tablespoon lemon juice
3 cups water	

Wash and dry the oranges. With a zester (a knifelike instrument with little holes) or vegetable peeler, remove half the zest of each orange, starting from the stem end and ending at the bottom, so that you end up with a striped orange. Be careful to remove just the zest and not the white pith. Keep the strips of zest to candy separately.

Using a very sharp, preferably serrated knife, starting from the bottom, slice each fruit into ⅛-inch slices. Discard the last thick slice with the stem.

Slightly overlap the slices on the oven rack. Set the oven to its lowest setting, about 175°F. (a ventilated oven works best). Let the slices dry in the oven for 1½ to 2 hours, until they feel almost dry and slightly sticky when touched.

Make the syrup. In a saucepan, simmer the sugar with 3 cups water and the cinnamon stick for about 30 minutes. Add the lemon juice and orange slices. Simmer for 6 to 10 minutes, until the slices start to look translucent. Remove the slices very carefully with tongs, letting the surplus syrup drain back into the pan. Pack the slices in a 3-cup jar.

Continue to simmer the syrup until it registers 220°F. on a candy thermometer. Pour the syrup over the orange slices and press them to submerge in the syrup. Cover, let cool, and store in the refrigerator.

Orange Slices in Syrup will keep for 2 to 3 months.

Makes 1½ pints.

VARIATION: After 1 to 2 days, drain some of the slices and let dry on a rack. Dredge in granulated sugar and let dry at room temperature or in a very low (175°F.) oven. Or, after drying the slices, dip them in melted bittersweet chocolate to make a delicious confection.

Pomegranate Jelly

Pomegranates are among the most celebrated fruits in the Mediterranean. Their many seeds symbolize fertility and prosperity, and for this reason Greeks break open a pomegranate in the entrance of houses, offices, and shops on the first day of each year.

Ancient Greeks used the sharp, tart-tasting juice of unripe pomegranates in many of the same ways we use lemon juice today. In this recipe, however, it is the tart-sweet taste of ripe pomegranates that is featured.

Serve Pomegranate Jelly instead of cranberry sauce, or use it to glaze roasts.

4–6 pomegranates, about 4 pounds or more
1 cinnamon stick, 2 inches long
2 tablespoons lemon juice
1 small beet, peeled and diced (optional; see Note)

Wearing a large apron (because the pomegranate juice can stain your clothes), score the outer skin of each pomegranate with a very sharp knife and peel it carefully. Remove and discard the inner yellow skin and collect the seeds in a large bowl.

Process the seeds in a food processor (all at once or in batches) until they are liquefied. Pass the pulp through a fine-meshed sieve lined with cheesecloth, pressing the pulp to extract all juices. You need about 4 cups of juice.

In a nonreactive saucepan, simmer the pomegranate juice for about 20 minutes. Add the cinnamon stick and lemon juice. Simmer for another 15 to 20 minutes, until the juice has thickened. Pour the hot juice through a strainer into a small glass jar, seal, and let cool.

Pomegranate Jelly will keep in the refrigerator for up to 6 months.

Makes about ½ cup.

NOTE: Some Middle Eastern recipes suggest that you use a small raw beet for color if your pomegranate seeds are very lightly colored. Add it to the juice along with the cinnamon stick.

Quince, Honey, and Sweet Wine Sauce

THIS FRAGRANT TART-SWEET SAUCE is an alternative to the more common cranberry and apple sauces. You can use it as a glaze with roasted poultry or game, or serve it alongside as a sauce. It is also great with Sautéed Manouri Cheese with Walnuts and Quince Sauce (see following page).

3–4 quinces (about 2¼ pounds), washed, dried, quartered, and cored, but not peeled

1½ cups sweet red wine, such as Mavrodaphne or port

6 whole cloves, tied in cheesecloth (optional)

1 cup sweet white wine, such as Samos Vin de Liqueur

5 tablespoons honey

2 tablespoons fresh lemon juice

With a sharp knife, halve and coarsely chop each quince quarter. Place in a nonreactive saucepan with 1 cup of the sweet red wine and the cloves (if you are using them) and simmer for 45 minutes, stirring from time to time.

Add ½ cup sweet white wine and the honey and simmer for another 10 to 15 minutes, until the mixture thickens slightly. Mash the fruit with a fork, add the remaining sweet white wine, and simmer, stirring often, for another 10 minutes.

Discard the cheesecloth with the cloves and transfer the cooked quince to a food processor and process to a smooth pulp. Return the pulp to the saucepan.

Add the remaining sweet red wine and the lemon juice to the saucepan and simmer for 20 to 35 minutes, stirring often, until all the liquid has evaporated.

Transfer to small jars and seal in a water bath (see page 15), or let cool and store in the refrigerator.

Quince, Honey, and Sweet Wine Sauce will keep for about 3 months.

Makes about 6 cups.

Sautéed Manouri Cheese with Walnuts and Quince Sauce

THIS UNUSUAL DESSERT was first created by Nikos Sarantos, the most talented chef in Greece. The recipe that follows is my own adaptation of his dish. If Manouri cheese is not available, use Ricotta Salata.

¼ cup ground walnuts

4 half-circle (⅓-inch-thick) slices Manouri cheese or Ricotta Salata

4 teaspoons butter or olive oil

16 walnut halves

½ cup Quince, Honey, and Sweet Wine Sauce (previous page)

Place the walnuts on a plate and press both sides of the cheese slices into them so that the cheese is coated with the nuts.

Warm the butter or oil in a heavy nonstick frying pan. Add the nut-coated cheese slices and sauté briefly, turning once, without letting the cheese melt. Meanwhile, warm the walnut halves under the broiler for about 2 minutes and the sauce in a double boiler.

Serve the sautéed cheese slices on warm plates. Decorate the cheese slices with the walnut halves and spoon the sauce around them.

Serves 4.

Walnuts in Honey

Honey mixed with nuts was one of the first desserts created before sugar became widely available in the 12th century. In fact, *honey* was synonymous with *sweet* for the Phoenicians, the ancient Greeks, the Romans, and all the other peoples who lived around the Mediterranean.

Even today, in *tavernas* in Crete and on other Greek islands, a small plate of walnuts and honey is brought to the table, usually as a complimentary offering by the restaurant owner. Walnuts with honey are also added to delicious, thick Greek yogurt to make a very nourishing breakfast or a quick dessert.

Almonds may be substituted for the walnuts in this recipe, but I think that walnuts are better with thyme-scented honey, which is the honey Greeks love most.

To serve, mix 2 to 3 tablespoons of the honey-coated walnuts into a cup of fresh, thick sheep's milk yogurt (see Mail-Order Sources, page 134).

⅔ cup walnuts, very coarsely crumbled by hand
Approximately 1 cup good-quality thick honey, preferably thyme-scented

Pack the walnuts in a 2-cup jar. Pour the honey over them to cover completely. Cover with the lid and keep in a cool dark place.

Walnuts in Honey will keep for 6 months to a year.

Makes about 2 cups.

I LEARNED ABOUT THESE quite unusual preserves from a Spanish lady who lives in Athens. We happened to be shopping at the same stand in my neighborhood farmer's market one winter morning, and we both bought a big piece of pumpkin. As it is quite rare for Athenians to cook this marvelous squash, I asked her what was she going to make with hers. "Preserves, of course. They are very common in Spain," she answered as she gave me her recipe. She then explained that these preserves can be served at breakfast, but she uses them mainly in her Pumpkin Tart (see page 129). You can use any kind of winter squash.

1 4-pound piece pumpkin, seeded	1 tablespoon whole cloves, tied in a piece of cheesecloth
3 cups sugar	1 tablespoon lemon juice

Preheat the oven to 375°F. Place the piece of pumpkin on a baking dish and bake for about 30 minutes, until tender.

With a spoon, scoop the soft pumpkin flesh away from the rind, then discard the rind. Transfer the pumpkin to a nonreactive saucepan. Add the sugar and cloves and simmer for 15 minutes, stirring with a wooden spoon, being careful not to let the mixture boil over. Add the lemon juice and cook a bit longer, until the preserves set. Discard the cheesecloth with the cloves.

Transfer the preserves to small, clean jars and close the lid.

Pumpkin Preserves will keep for about 3 months in the refrigerator.

Makes about 3½ cups.

Pumpkin Tart

⅓ cup olive oil

⅓ cup sunflower oil

½ cup sugar

2 eggs

3 tablespoons brandy

3–3½ cups unbleached all-purpose flour

1 teaspoon salt

½–1 teaspoon mixed ground cinnamon
  and cloves

Zest of 1 lemon

1½ cups Pumpkin Preserves (page 127)

⅔ cup slivered blanched almonds

OPPOSITE
Pumpkin Preserves

Place the olive and sunflower oils and the sugar in the bowl of a food processor and process for about 2 minutes. Add the eggs, brandy, 3 cups of the flour, salt, spice mixture, and lemon zest. Process again until you have a quite soft dough. If it is too soft, add a little more flour, being careful not to overwork the dough in the processor.

Divide the dough into 3 equal pieces, then form each piece into a ball, wrap in plastic wrap, and refrigerate for about 1 hour.

Preheat the oven to 375°F.

Lightly sprinkle a work surface and rolling pin with flour. Unwrap 2 pieces of dough, place one on top of the other, and roll into a circle at least 15 inches in diameter.

Lightly oil a 12-inch tart pan with a removable bottom and transfer the pastry to it. Trim the excess pastry from the edges and reserve. Pour the pumpkin preserves into the pastry shell and spread evenly with the back of a spoon.

Unwrap the remaining piece of pastry and combine with the excess pastry trimmed from the shell. Roll walnut-size pieces of pastry between your palms to obtain long thin cords, then crisscross the cords over the preserves to create a diamond pattern; press lightly on the ends to attach them to the rim of the pastry shell.

Sprinkle the tart with the almonds and bake for about 25 to 30 minutes, until golden brown. Let cool completely before removing from the tart pan and serving.

Serves 10.

Acknowledgments

I FEEL VERY PRIVILEGED to have been chosen by Leslie Stoker as one of Artisan's first authors and would like to thank her for showing such faith in my work.

I'm ever so grateful to Ann ffolliott, my editor and friend, for her penetrating comments and her enthusiasm for each new recipe, which she was always willing to try.

Many thanks to Jim Wageman for his brilliant design and to Hope Koturo, Sarah Scheffel, Melanie Falick, Laura Lindgren, and Carole Berglie, who helped in many ways to make this book possible.

I would like to express once more my gratitude to Martin Brigdale, the most gifted photographer I know, who always manages to create the pictures I have seen in my dreams. Martin and I would also like to convey our warmest thanks to Sophie Kelly, the talented painter and background artist, who worked tirelessly to create the atmosphere in those exquisite photographs. The very efficient Peter Cassidy, Martin's assistant, made sure that everything ran smoothly on those very long but rewarding days we spent in the studio. I would also like to express my thanks to Penny Markham for her remarkable prop styling.

The bulk of the recipes included in this book were collected over a period of many years during my travels, without a specific purpose other than to stock my own pantry with interesting items. For this reason I kept very few notes on the cooks from all over the Mediterranean and the friends and professional chefs who provided some of the original recipes. Nevertheless, I want to thank the friendly merchants in the Middle Eastern, North African, Spanish, French, Italian, Sicilian, Turkish, and, of course, Greek markets, as well as the women shopping for vegetables who stopped to explain their many uses in their part of the world. Also, I thank everyone who discussed, described, or gave me specific instructions on how to make spice mixtures, sauces, and all kinds of condiments, preserves, biscotti, and paximadia.

My special thanks to Paula Wolfert—who introduced me to the secrets of the North African pepper sauces—and was always available and helpful whenever I needed a deeper understanding of the cooking of the Mahgreb and the Middle East. Many thanks also to Carol Field, expert on Italian baking, for discussing biscotti and pane biscottato with me.

I would also like to thank Dun Gifford, Greg Dresher, and all the people at Oldways Preservation and Exchange Trust, for giving me the opportunity to meet such fascinating people during the conferences they have organized around the Mediterranean.

I'm grateful to the designer Athena Michael-Boutari who created the decorated aluminum plate in the photograph on page 72. The cast-iron incense burner, in the same picture, was my grandmother's and I would like to thank my cousin Leonidas Harvalias for offering it to me. Special thanks to Holly Lueders for the magnificent pleated silk scarves that appear in the photographs on pages 52–53 and 60.

Last but not least, I want to express my gratitude and thanks to my agent and friend Sarah Jane Freymann for her careful guidance and brilliant ideas.

Conversion Chart

Ingredients and Equipment Glossary

British English and American English are not always the same, particularly in the kitchen. The following ingredients and equipment used in this book are pretty much the same on both sides of the Atlantic, but have different names:

AMERICAN	BRITISH
arugula	rocket
beets	beetroots
bell pepper	sweet pepper (capsicum)
broiler/to broil	grill/to grill
charcoal grill	barbeque
chili peppers	chillis
confectioners' sugar	icing sugar
eggplant	aubergine
frying peppers	sweet peppers
scallion	spring onion
whole wheat	wholemeal
zucchini	courgette

Butter

Some confusion may arise over the measuring of butter and other hard fats. In the United States, butter is generally sold in a one-pound package, which contains four equal "sticks." The wrapper on each stick is marked to show tablespoons, so the cook can cut the stick according to the quantity required. The equivalent weights are:

1 stick = 115 g / 4 oz
1 T = 15 g / ½ oz

Flour

American all-purpose flour is milled from a mixture of hard and soft wheats, whereas British plain flour is made mainly from soft wheat. To achieve a near equivalent to American all-purpose flour, use half British plain flour and half strong bread flour.

American whole wheat flour is similar to British wholemeal flour.

Sugar

In the recipes in this book, if sugar is called for it is assumed to be granulated, unless otherwise specified. American granulated sugar is finer than British granulated, closer to caster sugar.

Oven Temperature Equivalents

Oven	°F.	°C.	Gas Mark
very cool	250–275	130–140	½–1
cool	300	150	2
warm	325	170	3
moderate	350	180	4
moderately hot	375	190	5
	400	200	6
hot	425	220	7
very hot	450	230	8
	475	250	9
	500	260	10

Volume Equivalents

These are not exact equivalents for the American cups and spoons, but have been rounded up or down slightly to make measuring easier.

American	Metric	Imperial
1¼ t	1.25 ml	
½ t	2.5 ml	
1 t	5 ml	
½ T (1½ t)	7.5 ml	
1 T (3 t)	15 ml	
¼ cup (4 T)	60 ml	2 fl. oz
⅓ cup (5 T)	75 ml	2½ fl oz
½ cup (8 T)	125 ml	4 fl oz
⅔ cup (10 T)	150 ml	5 fl oz (¼ pint)
¾ cup (12 T)	175 ml	6 fl oz
1 cup (16 T)	250 ml	8 fl oz
1¼ cups	300 ml	10 fl oz
1½ cups	350 ml	12 fl oz
1 pint (2 cups)	500 ml	16 fl oz
1 quart (4 cups)	1 litre	1¾ pints

Weight Equivalents

The metric weights given in this chart are not exact equivalents, but have been rounded up or down slightly to make measuring easier.

Imperial	Metric
¼ oz	7 g
½ oz	15 g
1 oz	30 g
2 oz	60 g
3 oz	90 g
4 oz	115 g
5 oz	150 g
6 oz	175 g
7 oz	200 g
8 oz (½ lb)	225 g
9 oz	250 g
10 oz	300 g
11 oz	325 g
12 oz	350 g
13 oz	375 g
14 oz	400 g
15 oz	425 g
16 oz	(1 lb) 450 g
1 lb 2 oz	500 g
1½ lb	750 g
2 lb	900 g
2¼ lb	1 kg
3 lb	1.4 kg
4 lb	1.8 kg
4½ lb	2 kg

Mail-Order Sources

Many of the distinctive ingredients used in Mediterranean cooking are available at farmers' markets, supermarkets, and ethnic grocery stores from Mediterranean countries. Attractive preserving bottles and jars are available at good houseware stores.

If you can't locate ingredients or containers, here are some places that provide mail-order service.

Adriana's Caravan
317 West 107th Street
New York, NY 10025
212/316-0820
800/316-0820
(mail-order only; catalogue available)

Near Eastern or Aleppo pepper, dried Mediterranean herbs and Greek oregano, mastic, mahlep, nigella, dried red and pink rose buds, saffron, sumac.

Aphrodisia Products, Inc.
264 Bleecker Street
New York, NY 10014
(catalogue available)
212/989-6440

Dried rose buds.

Dean and DeLuca
560 Broadway
New York, NY 10012
212/431-1691
800/221-7714

Near Eastern or Aleppo pepper, dried Mediterranean herbs, manouri cheese.

De Choix Specialty Foods Co.
58-25 52nd Avenue
Woodside, NY 11377
718/507-8080
800/332-4649
FAX 718/335-9150

Capers preserved in salt, saffron.

Hollow Road Farms
R.R. 1, Box 93
Stuyvesant, NY 12173
518/758-7214

Write for names of nearest suppliers of sheep's milk yogurt.

Kalustyan
123 Lexington Avenue
New York, NY 10016
(catalogue available)
212/685-3451

Near Eastern or Aleppo pepper, nigella, sumac.

Los Chileros de Nuevo Mexico
P.O. Box 6215
Santa Fe, NM 87502
505/471-6967

New Mexican chilies.

Oriental Pastry and Grocery
170–172 Atlantic Avenue
Brooklyn, NY 11201
718/875-7687

Near Eastern or Aleppo pepper, dried Mediterraean herbs, mastic, mahlep, sumac.

Paprikas Weiss Importer
1572 Second Avenue
New York, NY 10028
(catalogue available)
212/288-6117
FAX 212/734-5120

Mastic, dried Mediterranean herbs, sumac.

Pelopponese
6114 La Salle Avenue, #502
Oakland, CA 94611
510/547-7356

Greek olives.

Perfect Addition Rich Stock
P.O. Box 8976
Newport Beach, CA 92658
714/640-0220

Chicken stock.

Shallah's Middle Eastern Importing Company
290 White Street
Danbury, CT 06810
203/743-4181

Near Eastern or Aleppo pepper, mahlep, mastic, nigella, sumac.

Sultan's Delight
P.O. Box 090302
Brooklyn, NY 11209
(mail-order only; catalogue available)
718/745-6844
800/852-5046
FAX 718/745-2563

Mahlep, mastic, nigella, sumac.

Sur La Table
84 Pine Street
Seattle, WA 98101
(catalogue available)
206/448-2244

Ornamental bottles and jars.

Titan Foods
25-56 31st Street
Astoria, Queens, New York 11102
718/626-7771

Charcoal tablets for burning incense, mastic, Greek herbal teas, all kinds of Greek products.

Vanilla, Saffron Imports
949 Valencia Street
San Francisco, CA 94110
415/648-8990
FAX 800/334-2240

Saffron.

Williams-Sonoma
P.O. Box 7456
San Francisco, CA 94120
(catalogue available)
800/541-2233
FAX 415/421-5153

Bottles and jars, Saf-Instant Yeast.

For information about where to find Greek wines, olives, honey, and other products in your region, contact the:

Greek Food and Wine Institute
1114 Avenue of the Americas, 16th floor
New York, NY 10036
212/221-8000
FAX 212/221-8011

Bibliography

AFRC Institute of Food Research. *Home Preserva-tion of Fruit and Vegetables.* London: Her Majesty's Stationery Office, 1989.

Agapios, monk from Crete. *Greek folk medicine, nutrition, and agronomy in the beginning of the 18th century* (in Greek). 1850. Reprint. Athens: Cultura, 1979.

Algar, Ayla. *Classical Turkish Cooking.* New York: Harper Collins, 1991.

Andre, Jacques. *L'Alimentation et la cuisine a Rome.* Paris: Les belles lettres, 1981.

Ash, John. *American Game Cooking.* Reading, Mass.: Aris Books, 1991.

Athenaeus. *The Deipnosophists.* Loeb Classical Library. Cambridge, Mass.: Harvard University Press, 1971.

Bauman, Helmut. *Greek Wild Flowers.* London: Herbert Press, 1993.

Baysal, Ayse. *Samples from Turkish Cuisine.* Ankara: Turkish Historical Society, 1993.

Beard, James. *Beard on Bread.* New York: Alfred A. Knopf, 1981.

Blanc, Nicole and Anne Nercessian. *La cuisine Romaine Antique.* Paris: Glenat, Faton, 1982.

Bolens, Lucie. *La cuisine Andalouse, un Art de Vivre XI–XII siecle.* Paris: Albin Michel, 1990.

Castelvetro, Giacomo. *The Fruit, Herbs, and Veg-etables of Italy.* London: Viking, 1989.

David, Elizabeth. *A Book of Mediterranean Food.* London: Penguin, 1965.

———. *Summer Cooking.* London: Dorling Kindersley, 1988.

———. "Mad, mad, despised and dangerous." *Petits Propos Culinaires* 9. London: Prospect Books, 1981.

Davidson, Alan and Charlotte Knox. *Fruit, A Connoisseur's Guide and Cookbook.* London: Mitchell Beazley, 1991.

Edwards, John. *The Roman Cookery of Apicius.* Washington, D.C.: Hartley and Marks, 1984.

Efendi, Turabi. *Turkish Cookery Book.* 1862. Reprint. Sussex: Cook's Books, 1987.

Eren, Neset. *The Delights of Turkish Cooking.* Istanbul: Redhouse Yavinevi, 1988.

Field, Carol. *Celebrating Italy.* New York: William Morrow, 1990.

———. *The Italian Baker.* New York: Harper and Row, 1985.

———. *Italy in Small Bites.* New York: William Morrow, 1993.

Gedda, Guy. *La Table d'un Provençal.* Paris: Roland Escaing, 1989.

Gozzini, Giacosa Ilaria. *A Taste of Ancient Rome.* Chicago: University of Chicago Press, 1992.

Gray, Patience. *Honey from a Weed.* San Fran-cisco: North Point Press, 1990.

Hadjiat, Salima. *La Cuisine d'Algerie.* Paris: Pub-lisud, 1990.

Halici, Nevin. *Turkish Cookbook.* London: Dor-ling Kindersley, 1989.

Haroutunian, Arto der. *A Turkish Cookbook.* London: Ebury Press, 1987.

———. *Yogurt Book.* London: Penguin Books, 1984.

Hazan, Marcella. *The Essentials of Classic Italian Cooking.* London: Macmillan, 1992.

Heiser, Charles B., Jr. *Seed to Civilization: The Story of Food.* Cambridge, Mass.: Harvard University Press, 1990.

Helldreich, Theodore. *Dictionary of the Common Names of the Plants of Greece* (in Greek). Athens, 1980.

Herzberg, R., B. Vaughan, and J. Greene. *The New Putting Food By*. Brattleboro, Vermont: Stephen Greene Press, 1981.

Hill, Barbara. *The Cook's Book of Essential Information*. New York: Dell, 1987.

Imellos, Stefanos. "Looking at Food from a Folkloric Point of View" (in Greek). *Yearly Review of the Department of Philosophy*. Athens University. Vol. 28 (1979–1985) pp. 214–46.

Karaoglan, Aida. *Food for the Vegetarian: Traditional Lebanese Recipes*. New York: Interlink Books, 1988.

Kasper, Lynne Rossetto. *The Splendid Table*. New York: William Morrow, 1992.

Kavadas, Demetrios. *Botanical and Phytological Dictionary with Pictures* (in Greek). Athens, 1938.

Kokkinou, Marigoula and Georgia Kofina. *Lenten Meals and Desserts* (in Greek). Athens: Akdritas, 1988.

Kouki, Mohamed. *Cuisine et Patisserie Tunisiennes*. Tunis, 1987.

Lassalle, George. *East of Orphanides*. London: Kyle Cathie, Ltd., 1991.

Liacouras-Chantiles, Vilma. *The Food of Greece*. New York: Dodd, Mead and Co., 1985.

Liddell and Scott. *Greek-English Lexicon*. Oxford: Oxford University Press, 1969.

Lissen, A. and S. Cleary. *Tapas*. London: Apple Press, 1989.

Luard, Elisabeth. *Tapas*. Cambridge: Martin Books, 1991.

McGee, Harold. *The Curious Cook*. New York: Collier-Macmillan, 1992.

———. *On Food and Cooking*. London: Harper Collins, 1991.

Micha-Lampaki, Aspasia. "The appearance of specific foodstuffs in the traditional weddings of Boeotia" (in Greek). *Society of Boeotian Studies,* Vol. 1b (September 1986).

———. Bread as Bloodless Offering in Messinia, Peloponnese (in Greek). Athens, *Society of Peloponnesian Studies,* 1984.

Packman, Sue. *Foods Preserved*. London: Cassel, 1992.

Pappas, Lou Seibert. *Biscotti*. San Francisco: Chronicle Books, 1992.

Perna Bozzi, Ottorina. *Vecchia Milano in Cucina*. Florence: Giunti Martello, 1975.

Ramazanoglu, Gulseren. *Turkish Cooking*. Istanbul: Ramazanoglu Publications, 1992.

Rayess, George. *The Art of Lebanese Cooking*. Beirut: Librarie du Liban, 1982.

Recipe Club of Saint Paul's Greek Orthodox Cathedral. *The Complete Book of Greek Cooking*. New York: Harper and Row, 1990.

Rinzler, Carol Ann. *Herbs, Spices, and Condiments*. New York: Henry Holt & Co., 1990.

Riddervold, Astri and Andreas Ropeid. *Food Conservation, Ethnological Studies*. London: Prospect Books, 1988.

Roden, Claudia. *The Food of Italy*. London: Arrow Books, 1990.

———. *Mediterranean Cookery*. London: BBC Books, 1992.

———. *A New Book of Middle Eastern Food*. London: Penguin, 1963.

Schneider, Elizabeth. *Uncommon Fruits and Vegetables: A Commonsense Guide*. New York: Harper Perennial, 1990.

Senderens, Alain. *Figues sans barbarie*. Paris: Robert Laffont, 1991.

Simeti, Mary Taylor. *On Persephone's Island*. San Francisco: North Point Press, 1986.

———. *Pomp and Sustenance*. New York: Henry Holt & Co., 1991.

Spicing Up the Palate: Proceedings of the Oxford Symposium on Food and Cookery 1992. London: Prospect Books, 1992.

Stathaki-Koumari, Rodoula. *The Traditional Bread of Rethymnon* (in Greek). Rethymnon: The Rethymnon Museum of History and Folk Tradition, 1983.

Stavroulakis, Nicholas. *Cookbook of the Jews of Greece*. New York: Cadmus Press, 1986.

Stobart, Tom. *Herbs, Spices, and Flavorings*. Woodstock, New York: The Overlook Press, 1970.

Tamzali, Haydee. *La cuisine en Afrique du Nord*. Tunis: Michael Tomkinson, 1990.

Tolley, Emily and Chris Mead. *The Herbal Pantry*. New York: Clarkson Potter, 1992.

Torres, Marimar. *A Catalan Country Kitchen*. Reading, Mass.: Aris Books, 1992.

Traditional Greek Recipes (in Greek). 6 vols. Athens: Fytrakis, n.d.

Thesaurus Linguae Graecae (CD ROM). Irvine: University of California, 1987.

Tselementes, Nicholas. *Cooking and Patisserie Guide* (in Greek). 1920. Reprint. Athens: Fytrakis, 1983.

Waines, David. *In a Caliph's Kitchen*. London: Rad el Rayyes Books, 1989.

Waycott, Edon. *Preserving the Taste*. New York: Hearst Books, 1993.

Wells, Patricia. *Bistro Cooking*. New York: Workman, 1989.

Witty, Helen. *Fancy Pantry*. New York: Workman, 1986.

Wolfert, Paula. *The Cooking of the Eastern Mediterranean*. New York: Harper Collins, 1994.

———. *Couscous and Other Good Food from Morocco*. New York: Harper Perennial, 1989.

———. *Mediterranean Cooking*. New York: Ecco Press, 1985.

———. *Paula Wolfert's World of Food*. New York: Harper and Row, 1988.

Unknown man from Pelion. *Notebook on Nutrition, Botany and Agriculture* (in Greek). Annotated and edited by G. Sfikas. Athens, 1991.

Index

DESIGNED BY JIM WAGEMAN

TYPEFACES IN THIS BOOK ARE
MONOTYPE DANTE, DESIGNED BY GIOVANNI MARDERSTEIG,
AND CHARLEMAGNE, DESIGNED BY CAROL TWOMBLY
THE TYPE WAS SET BY LAURA LINDGREN, NEW YORK

PRINTED AND BOUND BY
TOPPAN PRINTING COMPANY, LTD.
TOKYO, JAPAN